Contents

Director's Foreword

We are thrilled to welcome back the *Taylor Wessing Photo Portrait Prize* for 2024. Each year, the competition showcases contemporary portraits by talented photographers from around the world. This year we received a total of 4,847 entries by 1,713 photographers from 50 countries. We are delighted that the competition has increased its reach, having received entries from countries that have not previously entered, including Nepal, Peru and Sudan.

The judges saw an increased focus on family, community and identity depicted within the submissions. The shortlisted 62 photographs draw attention to important causes and themes through unique compositions, crops and settings. They were carefully chosen by our judges through an anonymous process that allowed for focus to remain firmly on each photograph's unique qualities and merits. My thanks go to this year's judges, Clare Freestone, Pogus Caesar, Alona Pardo and Lou Stoppard, for their collaborative and insightful approach.

My congratulations go to the four prizewinners. Steph Wilson received first prize for a photograph taken from her series *Ideal Mother*, displaying an intimate portrayal of unconventional motherhood. Second prize was awarded to Adam Ferguson for his ambitious project that attempts to dispel sentimental and outdated narratives around the Outback by considering issues such as colonial legacy and the impacts of globalisation. Tjitske Sluis received third prize for a photograph of her mother, conveying themes of vulnerability, love and mortality. This year, Jesse Navarre Vos has been awarded the Taylor Wessing Photographic Commission, for his quiet and sensitive portrait of his mother, who is in fact his biological grandmother, taken from a series entitled *Mom, I'll Follow You Still*.

Our In Focus Photographer is Diana Markosian, an American-Russian contemporary artist of Armenian descent. For the first time, Markosian will be exhibiting work from her series *Father*. The work mirrors the familial intimacy seen within the Prize's final submissions. Her documentary storytelling explores the artist's journey in tracing her estranged father in Armenia, his search for his lost children and their developing relationship.

I extend my thanks to the staff at the National Portrait Gallery, Grade Design for their work on the exhibition catalogue, the White Wall Company for their management of the judging process, and Taylor Wessing for their continued support of the Prize.

Victoria Siddall
Director, National Portrait Gallery, London

Sponsor's Foreword

This is another record-breaking milestone for the *Taylor Wessing Photo Portrait Prize*. The competition has attracted nearly 5,000 entries from over 1,700 photographers in 50 countries. Quality and variety are showcased in the entries submitted by talented photographers from around the globe.

We are proud to be a longstanding partner of the Photo Portrait Prize, now in its seventeenth year, and to recognise the creativity and excellence of contemporary photographers. Among the multitude of entries received this year, historical processes have been utilised, such as the tintype (a photograph made directly onto a sheet of metal), and there are depictions ranging from well-known figures to contemplative portraits of family members. The varying submissions highlight the global and cultural reach of the Prize. All of them are powerful and thought-provoking images that will delight viewing audiences.

We are particularly excited to support the continuation of the Taylor Wessing Photographic Commission into its second year. This provides a further opportunity for one photographer to be recognised, with their new commission added to the National Portrait Gallery's permanent collection – a fantastic accolade for any artist.

I hope you will enjoy the 2024 exhibition and join Taylor Wessing in celebrating the exceptional talent of the photographers showcased.

Shane Gleghorn
Taylor Wessing Managing Partner

The Judges

Alona Pardo
Curator

It was a pleasure and a privilege to be part of this year's panel for the *Taylor Wessing Photo Portrait Prize*, which I have followed avidly over the last decade. The portraits submitted reflected intimacy and vulnerability, while representing and celebrating the diversity of our global communities with tenderness and power. The process forces each judge to study the shortlisted works carefully, and I thoroughly enjoyed the lively and robust debate between the judges and was impressed by the calibre of work submitted.

Lou Stoppard
Writer and Curator

I enjoyed judging this year's Prize. In my opinion, great portraits offer some kind of glimpse into the depth of a life lived. I was happy to see that many of the submissions captured their subjects as multifaceted beings – avoiding the allure of pure visual impact or simplistic messaging, to instead engage with portraiture that lingers in the mind rather than just what grabs the eye. People are always more than one thing, and the portraits that reflect that complexity – the contradictions flourishing within all of us – are the ones that stand out to me.

Pogus Caesar
Multimedia Artist

Throughout my photographic career, I am constantly evolving and learning how to produce better photographs. So, it has been a joyous experience judging this year's Prize. A dazzling display of photographs were submitted, propelling me on a visual voyage into the lens of highly creative individuals. In my opinion, the photographs I have encountered are historic and culturally valuable documents. More importantly, they open a door into a world revealing the existence of those communities we may never encounter or embrace.

Clare Freestone
National Portrait Gallery Curator, Photography

It was an honour, after many years of observing the Prize, to be one of the judges. The entrants demonstrate the continued quality and diversity of approaches to photographic portraiture. This rich selection emerged after an intoxicating judging process reflecting upon these unique visual interpretations of personal and universal concerns.

The Prizes

First Prize

Steph Wilson

Wilson's portrait challenges the conventional portrayal of motherhood through an intimate revelation of identity (p.6).

Second Prize

Adam Ferguson

In *Big Sky*, Ferguson counters romanticised views of Australian Indigenous communities (p.8).

Third Prize

Tjitske Sluis

Portraying her mother in a vulnerable moment, Sluis reflects on the complexity of end of life care (p.12).

Taylor Wessing
Photographic Commission

Jesse Navarre Vos

Vos explores how photography can help one to navigate familial relationships during difficult periods (p.14).

The *Taylor Wessing Photo Portrait Prize* is open to photographers from around the world, aged 18 or over. Exhibited annually at the National Portrait Gallery, London, the Prize showcases talented photographers, both professional and amateur. The winner of the competition receives £15,000, with second prize receiving £3,000 and third prize £2,000. In addition, the National Portrait Gallery awards an £8,000 Taylor Wessing Photographic Commission, which will see a photographer selected to create a work for the Gallery's Collection.

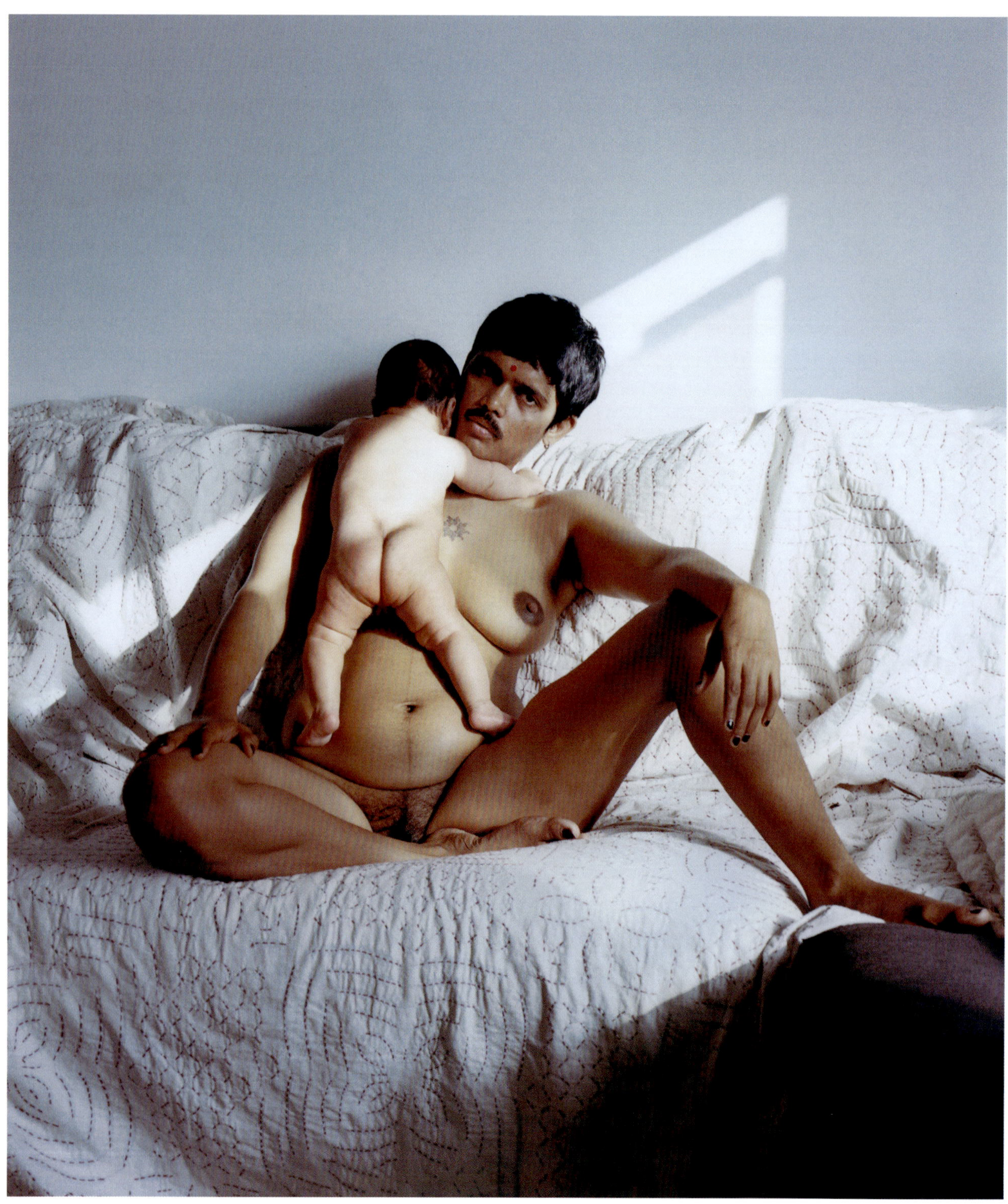

Steph Wilson
Sonam, 2023
From the series *Ideal Mother*
Inkjet print

First Prize
Steph Wilson

Sonam extends herself on her sofa while her newborn grapples with her body, feet poised lightly on Sonam's thigh and stomach, the raking light through the window falling across a small section of both of their naked bodies. This portrait of early motherhood is the result of a casting call via Instagram by photographer Steph Wilson for an ongoing book project. Wilson was compelled to broaden the existing aesthetics and visual language of pregnancy by focusing on what can sometimes dismissively be referred to as 'socially atypical mothers'.

Wilson's inspiration for the book came from a shoot for *Riposte* magazine, where she was commissioned to photograph pregnant people. The sitters were contacted through an open call, and Wilson remembers the response encompassing conventional depictions of motherhood. In a bid to subvert this cycle of representation and to embrace all types of beauty, she has spent nearly three years in pursuit of this vulnerable and revealing project.

Wilson's path to photography stemmed from an early painting career, while her focus on representation and allyship is informed by her work in fashion photography, where she works to reassert power balances between photographer and model and in the types of beauty she seeks to represent. Her practice is infused by her love of painterly tactility. She shoots on film and hand prints from the negative – which she sees as key in conceptualising the final portrait.

Sonam's direct, unsmiling gaze at the camera lens unsettles expectations. Her wide legged sprawl and close cut hair and moustache make for an unexpectedly masculine image of motherhood. The nudity is also a subversion; it is not a meek or apologetic study of the female form. Sonam is pictured with presence, taking up space within the domestic context. Wilson chooses to elicit a sense of ease and comfort when working with sitters to allow for their own self-reflection: 'It felt special portraying someone really trusting and explicit in the fact that they felt comfortable.'

Wilson's ambition was to present sitters as more than just their pregnancies. Hence, the intentional introduction to Sonam's profession as a wig maker. The moustache is not simply a reference to her career, but also alludes to Sonam's other possible identities that can exist beyond motherhood. The prop, a replica of her father's moustache, represents a third generation in this unconventional family portrait. It also harkens back to her childhood when friends and family would remark on her masculine features, that long hair did not suit her, and tell her to embrace her naturally occurring self.

Wilson reflects that in an age of visual saturation and ease of duplication, how persuasive it is 'to be taken by surprise by an image.' The photograph is a powerful representation of a broader spectrum of pregnancy, birth, parenthood and sense of self. Beyond the masculine traits the eye may immediately be drawn towards, there are a number of other easily overlooked details. Sonam's painted nails and small hoop earrings are discreet, typically read as feminine markers. They actively acknowledge her choice of self-representation through the combination of masculine and feminine. Sonam accentuates this further, with the bindi as a symbol to 'highlight the feminine culture from my motherland.'

This is a portrait of balance, of blending, and of broadening conversations on pregnancy and parenthood. It is also a visual reminder that people can assimilate many seemingly contradictory characteristics in the pursuit of individuality and authenticity.

Interview by Mariama Attah

Second Prize
Adam Ferguson

Adam Ferguson turned to photography out of the disillusionment he felt as a teenager living in Coffs Harbour, Australia. A strong environmental conscience, and a chance meeting with a photographer while surfing, led him to pick up his mother's Pentax K1000 and apply to the Queensland College of Art and Design, Brisbane, Australia. Influenced by his lecturer David Lloyd, it was here that he was introduced to his love of documentary photography, through the work of Don McCullin, Henri Cartier-Bresson and Eugene Richards – 'and I just knew I was going to be a photojournalist or documentary photographer'.

Ferguson's camera became a tool to express feelings of 'exclusion and discontent.' Anti-war and anti-imperialist – 'I knew from that first semester that I wanted to cover conflicts'. Graduating in 2004, Ferguson began photographing environmental portraits. He gained an internship with the international VII Photo Agency, and founding member Gary Knight became his most significant mentor. In 2008, he moved to New Delhi and amid the hub of international news organisations he gained assignments. Later that year, Ferguson self-funded his first trip to Afghanistan. He achieved his first *Time* magazine cover story in 2009, and further commissions, covering the conflict 'intensely'.

'Photojournalism is reactive coverage of the real events and is important to our understanding of the world, but there's something powerful in taking time to engage with an individual and have them collaborate and make a story, through portraiture.'

He refers to his recently published project *Big Sky,* for which the three prizewinning portraits were made. Photographing the inhabitants of Australia's romanticised Outback, it was essential 'to hear their story and make creative decisions that responded to the integrity of that story.' Influenced by Richard Avedon's *In the American West,* Ferguson, 'embarked on this body of work

in an attempt to understand a place I had left behind. My family history epitomised a social fabric that was once enmeshed with iconic bush towns. The country's occupation and colonial legacy has meant a deep dispossession of traditional custodians from their lands, language and culture. And while the modern Australian state has progressed, the land has been plundered.'

The series, photographed over a ten-year period, depicts the impacts of globalisation and the adversity of climate change. The images were made during extended journeys into the Northern Territory and Western Australia. In *Kukatja Pintupi boy Matthew West, hunting trip,* Ferguson captures a defiance and agency in the spontaneous gesture of the boy presenting him with a dead joey, a by-product of a kangaroo hunt near the remote community of Balgo, Western Australia. The photographer sees this image as a critique of the death and destruction that Western settlers have inflicted. For Ferguson, it also represents the importance of permission from elders and sensitivity to Indigenous communities, which is integral to Ferguson's photographic practice.

Ferguson met Simon Dixon, a Lutheran pastor, at an Easter church service in Haasts Bluff, Northern Territory, and returned to make the portrait in consultation with him and the church. The Lutheran missionaries who established Christian communities in this remote part of the country a century ago transformed the nomadic life of Indigenous populations. Ferguson intentionally juxtaposed the exalting pastor in his robes with the uncultivated landscape behind.

Another powerful dissimilitude is the idolised global popstar Taylor Swift, emblazed on the backs of Bridget and Shauna - 'an unplanned portrait'. The young Indigenous women sit overlooking the vast bush landscape; 'Bridget turned around and I made this picture.' It is the gaze of the young

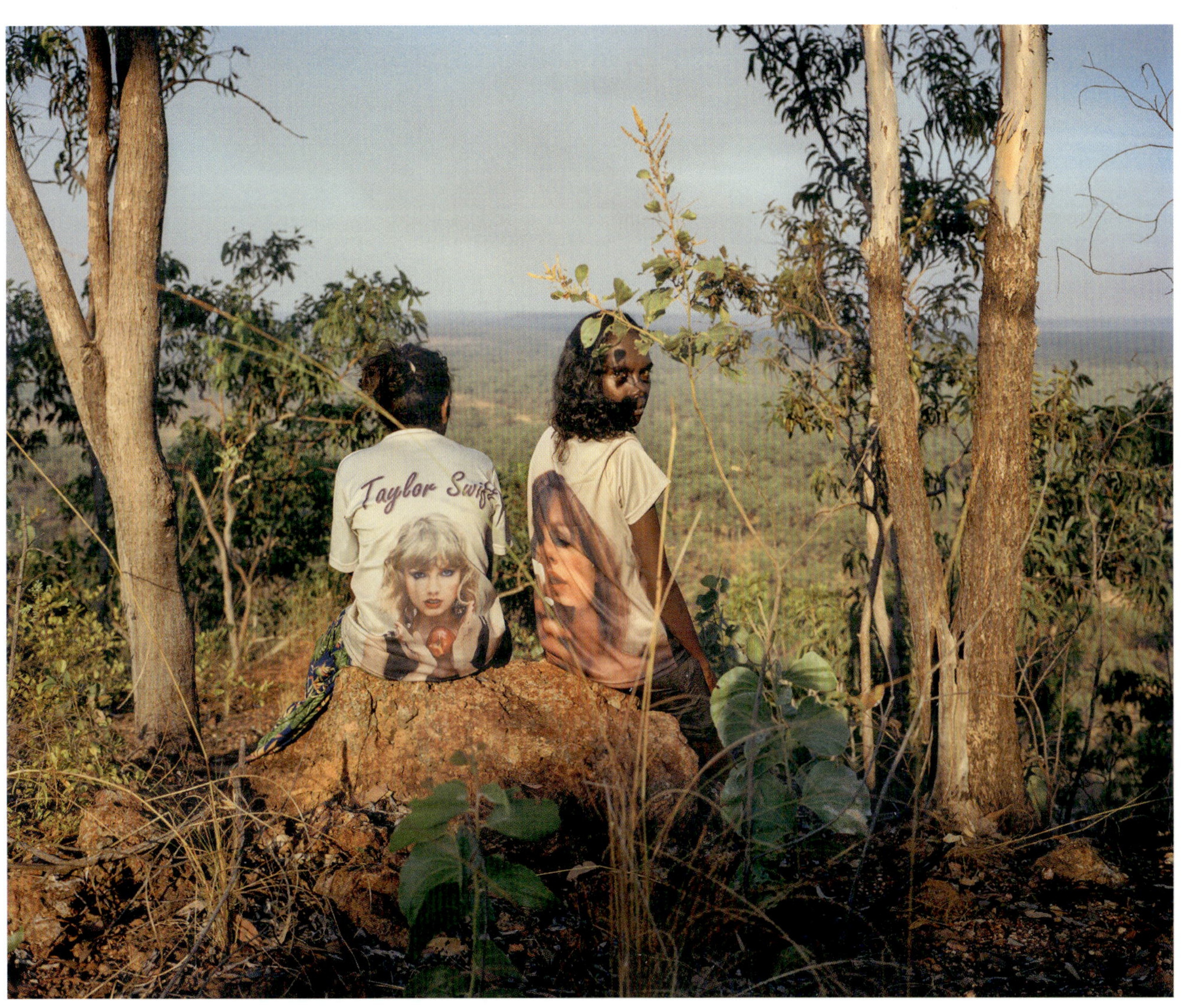

Adam Ferguson
Cousin sisters Shauna and Bridget Perdjert,
Kardu Thithay Diminin Clan and Murrinhpatha
language group, Kardu Yek Diminin Country,
Air Force Hill, Wadeye, Northern Territory, 2023
From the series *Big Sky*
Inkjet print

Adam Ferguson
Pintupi-Luritja Lutheran Pastor Simon Dixon,
Ikuntji/Haasts Bluff, Arrernte Country,
Northern Territory, 2023
From the series *Big Sky*
Inkjet print

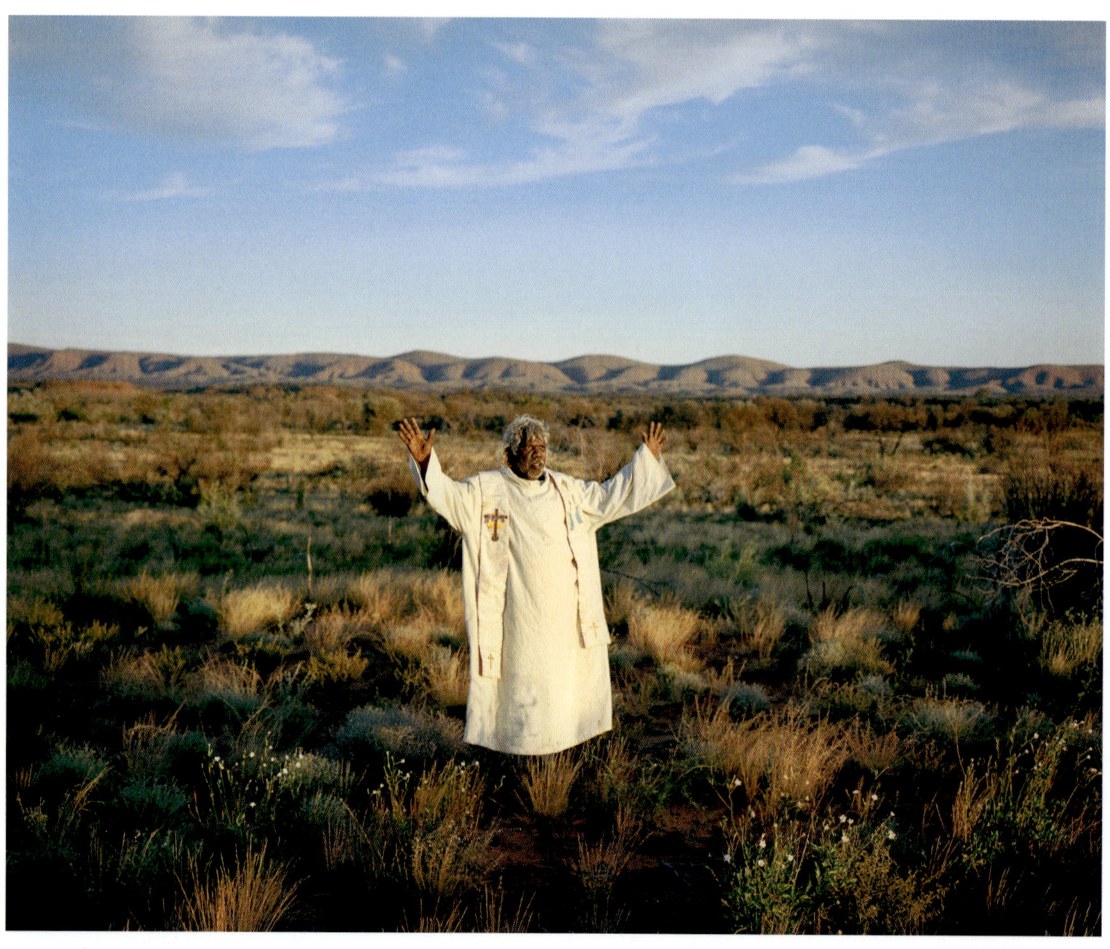

woman, a 'Swiftie', which adds to the success of the portrait as an identifier of pervading commercialisation. The reality of life contrasts with the romantic fantasy depicted in history and popular culture. 'A big part of my work is about exploring that tension.' Ferguson shoots on analogue medium format, partly as an aesthetic choice and to counter the expendable nature of digital, but primarily 'it required me to slow down and really think about every photograph that I made.'

Ferguson is currently an MFA research candidate looking at his conflict archive through a critical lens and staging interventions to form a new body of work. His desire to observe the reality of his country and dispel myths through photography is also undiminished. Ferguson concludes; 'I don't think I can stop photographing regional Australia. It's something that I have inside of me.'

Interview by Clare Freestone

Adam Ferguson
Kukatja Pintupi boy Matthew West, hunting trip,
Wirrimanu/Balgo, Kukatja Country,
Western Australia, 2023
From the series Big Sky
Inkjet print

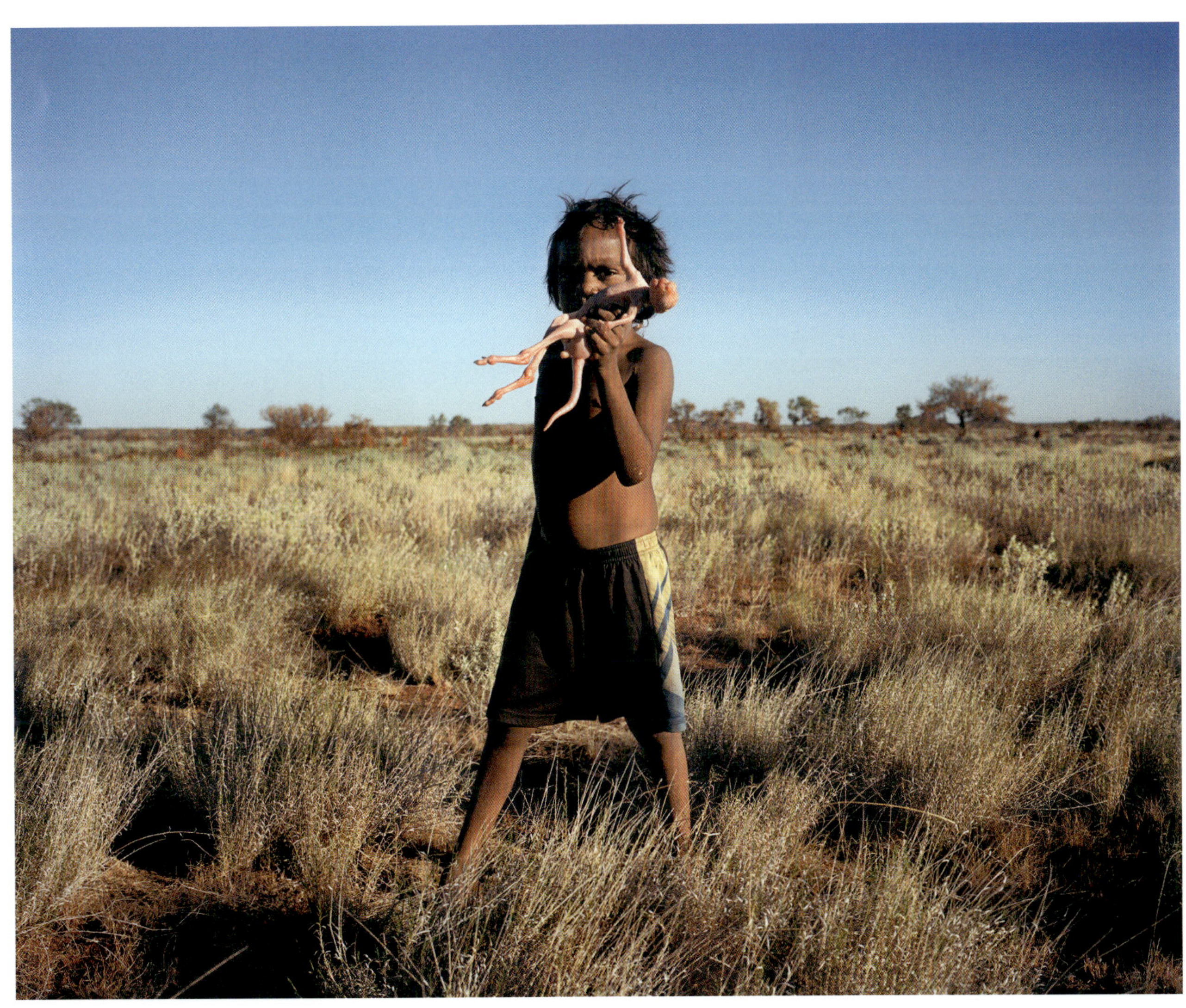

Third Prize
Tjitske Sluis

Tjitske Sluis did not plan to create a portrait series about her mother Teuntje's last stage of life. When she became Teuntje's full-time carer in 2021, she did not know when she would pick up a camera again.

Sluis came to photography through journalism. At the Dutch newspaper *Dagblad De Limburger*, she found herself drawn to the storytelling power of photographs, the immediacy of images over words. A career in reportage followed, balanced with raising a family. Eventually, Sluis decided to go freelance as a documentary photographer, but then her mother became sick.

Caring for a parent at their end of life is a disorientating experience, with grief accompanied by a destabilising reversal of roles. Teuntje – always independent – drew inwards after her diagnosis, whilst Sluis struggled with the barrage of emotional and domestic labour. To cope, she reached for her camera, using documentary photography to understand the events unfolding around her. Teuntje found a tension-relieving humour in being photographed: 'I would show her a picture and she would say, "Oh, I want that printed big on my coffin".'

Sluis's portrait of her sleeping mother, afloat on a sea of floral duvet, speaks to the deep trust and understanding between them. Tender details reflect Teuntje's mental resilience in the face of declining physical health. Despite her frail form, Teuntje's 'essence and infectious spirit' is echoed through her bold lip-patterned jumper and the dog's bright eyes.

It is a portrait that only Sluis, as a daughter and carer, could make. Yet, the elevated perspective creates distance from the scene. Adopting a documentary approach allowed Sluis to 'catch my breath back again' during overwhelming moments. 'It is like zoning out into your professional mode ... doing what you are good at, and then zoning back into the situation with renewed energy.'

Sluis's portrait acted as a waypoint, 'That was the night I decided I was not going to go home.' Reflecting on this moment of realisation, the distinctions between Sluis's roles as daughter, carer and photographer start to slip: 'What you need as a documentary photographer is antennas. You need to be able to tune in on someone. I do not know if it is something she said or something she did ... I just looked at her and I thought, I am not going to leave.'

Teuntje passed away a fortnight after this portrait was taken. With support from a photographer friend, Sluis began editing. This intensely challenging process helped her to come to terms with her grief. It also gave rise to an anger at the lack of care support available to families in the Netherlands. *Out of Love, Out of Necessity* points to a healthcare crisis of overcrowded care homes and a shortage of professional care workers. When family members are consumed with cleaning, feeding and washing, you are unable to simply 'drink a proper cup of coffee with your dying mother', Sluis explains.

Despite the challenges, Sluis was determined to help her mother die at home, on her own terms. In turn, her photographs helped to raise awareness. *Out of Love, Out of Necessity* was published by the Dutch newspaper *de Volkskrant*, and it prompted debates in Dutch parliament about end of life care. Empowered to use her photography to bring about meaningful change, Sluis is now pursuing a master's degree in care ethics.

For Sluis, gaining recognition for the series is bittersweet. It is also a fitting eulogy to her mother's infectious spirit, 'She would have been so proud. She always believed in my photography from the moment I grabbed a camera ... I think this may be a crown for her'.

Interview by Ruby Rees-Sheridan

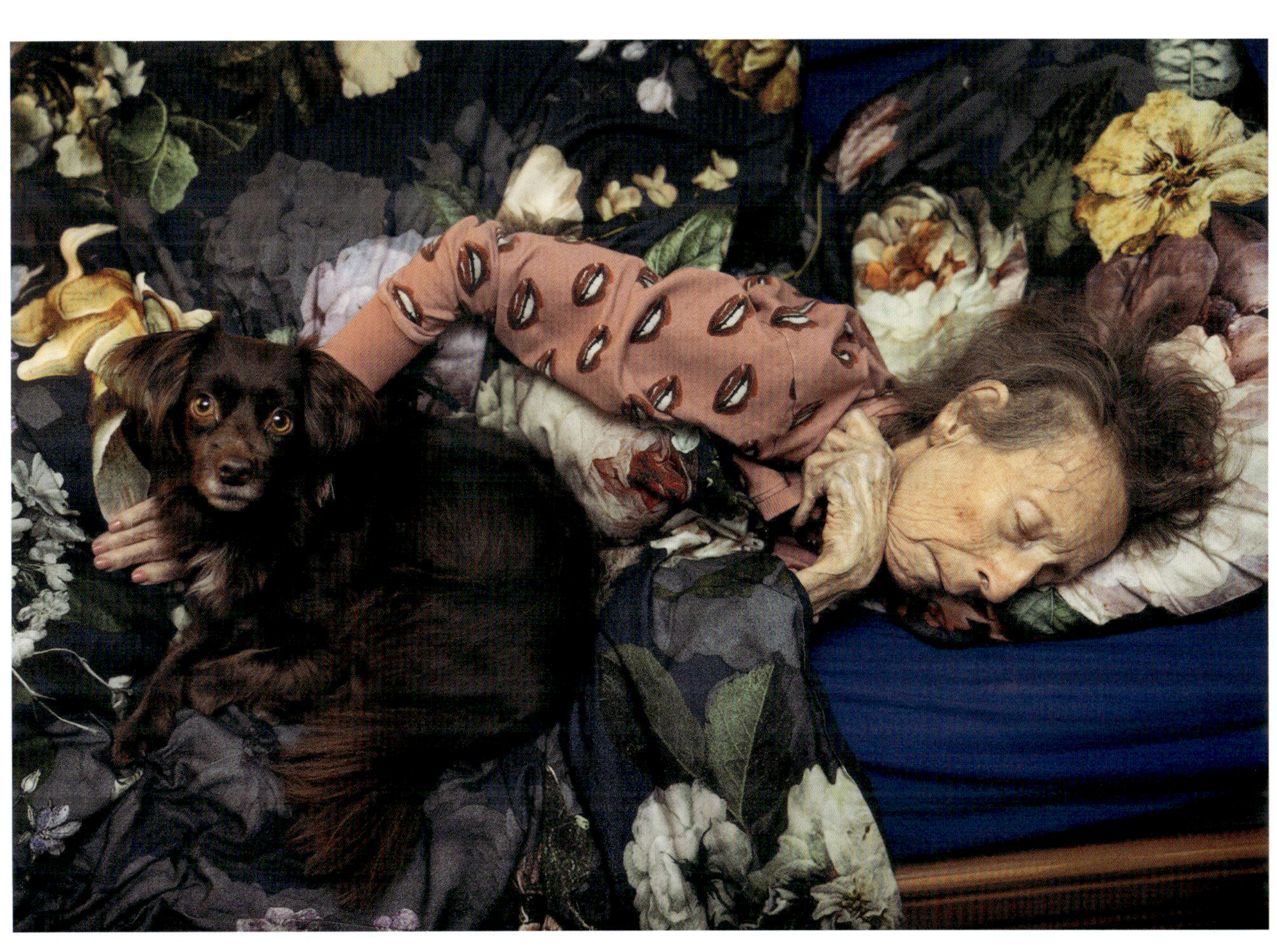

Tjitske Sluis
Mom, 2023
From the series *Out of Love, Out of Necessity*
Inkjet print

Taylor Wessing Photographic Commission
Jesse Navarre Vos

Jesse Navarre Vos is the second recipient of the Taylor Wessing Photographic Commission. Seeing portrait photography as a way of connecting with people, Vos has straddled several genres: from fashion and editorial to the ongoing personal collaboration with his mother.

Born in 1991, Cape Town, South Africa, Vos studied music before completing a bachelors degree in Anthropology and History. Having developed a love of the darkroom at school, and enjoying engaging with narrative, Vos revisited photography after almost a decade at the age of 25. He borrowed two cameras from a friend and embarked on a road trip across South Africa. This was a turning point in Vos's practice; 'Since then I haven't really put a camera down'.

Photography became a visual tool that could co-exist with other means of expression: writing, film and music. It is a line from Cat Power's live rendition of Bob Dylan's 'Mr Tambourine Man', 'in the jingle jangle morning I'll come following you', that titles Vos's current project. Central to this series is Edith, the photographer's mother, who is in fact his biological paternal grandmother. She has been his legal guardian since Vos's birth and mother by adoption since his teens.

In 2018, a burglary at Vos's family home triggered the narrative of 'ambiguous loss.' Edith 'lost herself. I lost her. The search began.' His formerly self-reliant mother became unable to look after herself. She passed into Vos's care, then into a temporary nursing home, before entering the care facility seen in Vos's winning image *Mom, I'll follow you still*. COVID-19 restrictions had added a 'further layer of distance' between them. 'I started following her around the empty rooms, corridors, passages … all seemingly leading nowhere, as there was nowhere to go to. The idea of following her arrived through my attempts to preserve her.'

At this challenging time, Vos paused his pursuit of an artistic career and returned to university to study psychology. Yet, he continued to photograph his mother. 'Over the years the narrative started coming through'. In 2023, Vos sought a mentorship with British photographer Siân Davey, and at the beginning of this year he participated in an intimate online group workshop with Diana Markosian (this year's In Focus Photographer).

Alongside these photographers, whose biographical projects share connections with Vos's, he cites several writers that have informed his work, including W. G. Sebald, Natasha Trethewey, Saidiya Hartman, and Ocean Vuong. Vos states, 'my intention is to create a work that transcends mere documentation, aiming instead to capture the essence of our relationship and the transformations we have both undergone.'

Vos sees the camera as a 'vehicle for telling stories' but the choice of equipment as informing 'aesthetic sensibility'. Normally favouring medium format film, recently Vos has used a large format camera to photograph his mother in *Mom, I'll follow you still*. These choices 'change how you engage. Large format forces me to slow down, especially when photographing people, it is important to create some sense of a connection.' Vos responds to the environment rather than staging sittings, and concludes that he has always had 'an intense fascination with people and stories. I think that is what underlies this.'

When photographing his mother in the lift, he felt she was 'distant, going somewhere that I could not follow.' In pausing to make the image, propping the door open with a cushion, he sustained the connection. This project is a collaboration; his mother an equal contributor who reflects on the photographs and enjoys the recognition they bring.

Interview by Clare Freestone

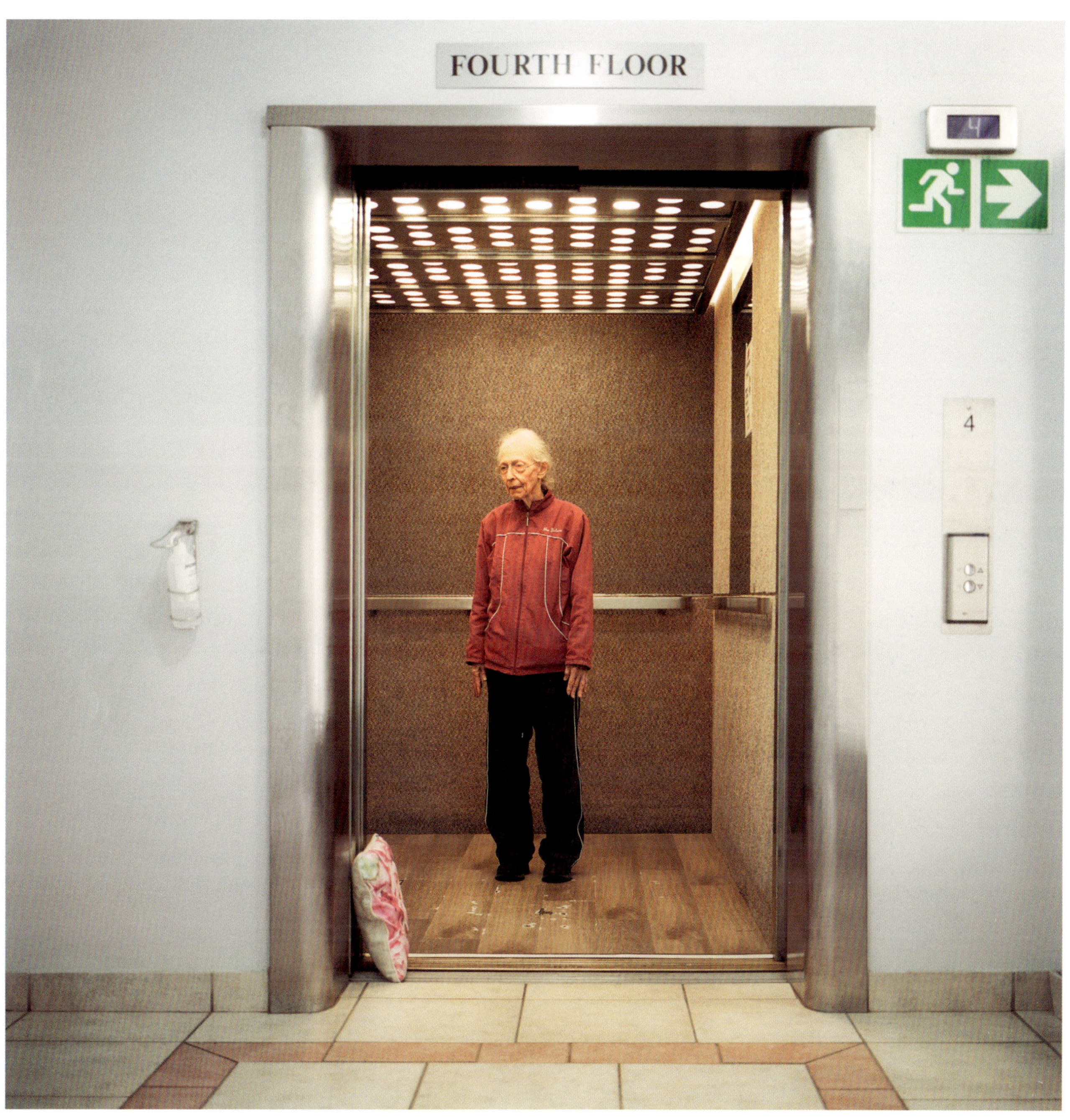

Jesse Navarre Vos
Mom, I'll follow you still, 2023
From the series *I'll come following you*
Chromogenic print

Exhibitors

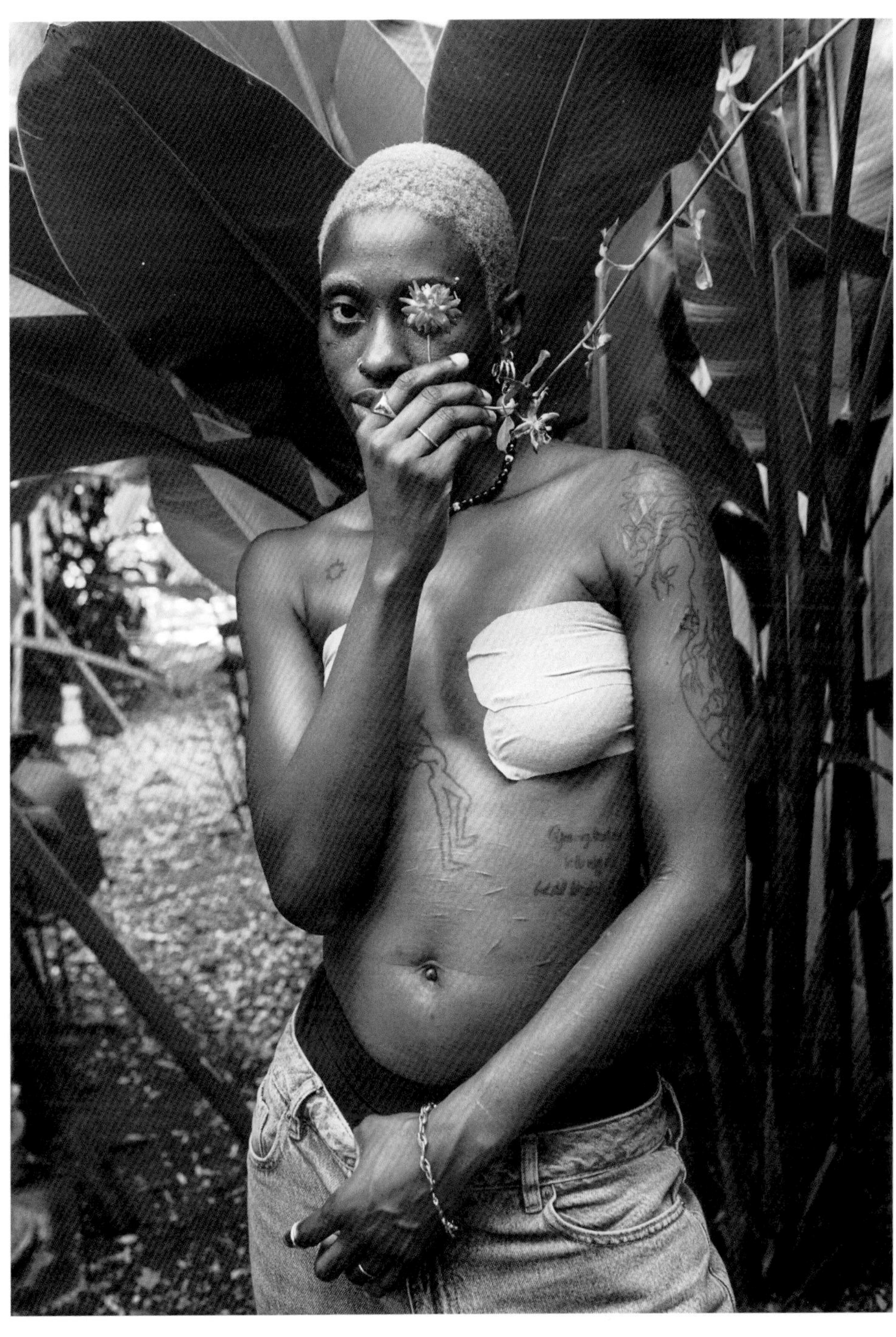

Janice Reid
Portrait of Afé, 2023
Inkjet print

Portrait of Afé gives a glimpse into the journeys made and memories accumulated over time, within a Black trans body. There is reference to religions and spiritualities which embrace and acknowledge broader ways of living and thriving, against a backdrop of towering plant life. Janice Reid asks us to consider the long established presence of queerness in nature and questions: 'when the flesh dies, what does your spirit look and feel like?'

Tadhg Joseph

Untitled, 2023
From the series *The Adoption Albums*
Chromogenic print

This portrait of Tadhg Joseph's father Mark is part of an ongoing collaboration. Joseph's parents adopted him from foster care, and through this project he explores the role that photography played following his adoption. The series is inspired by the photographs that Joseph's parents made to devise a 'family album'. Through the restaging of memories, the collaboration calls into question the participation of father and son and how images are constructed. This portrait was made on a trip to Inishnee, Ireland, where Joseph's paternal grandmother and great-grandmother lived.

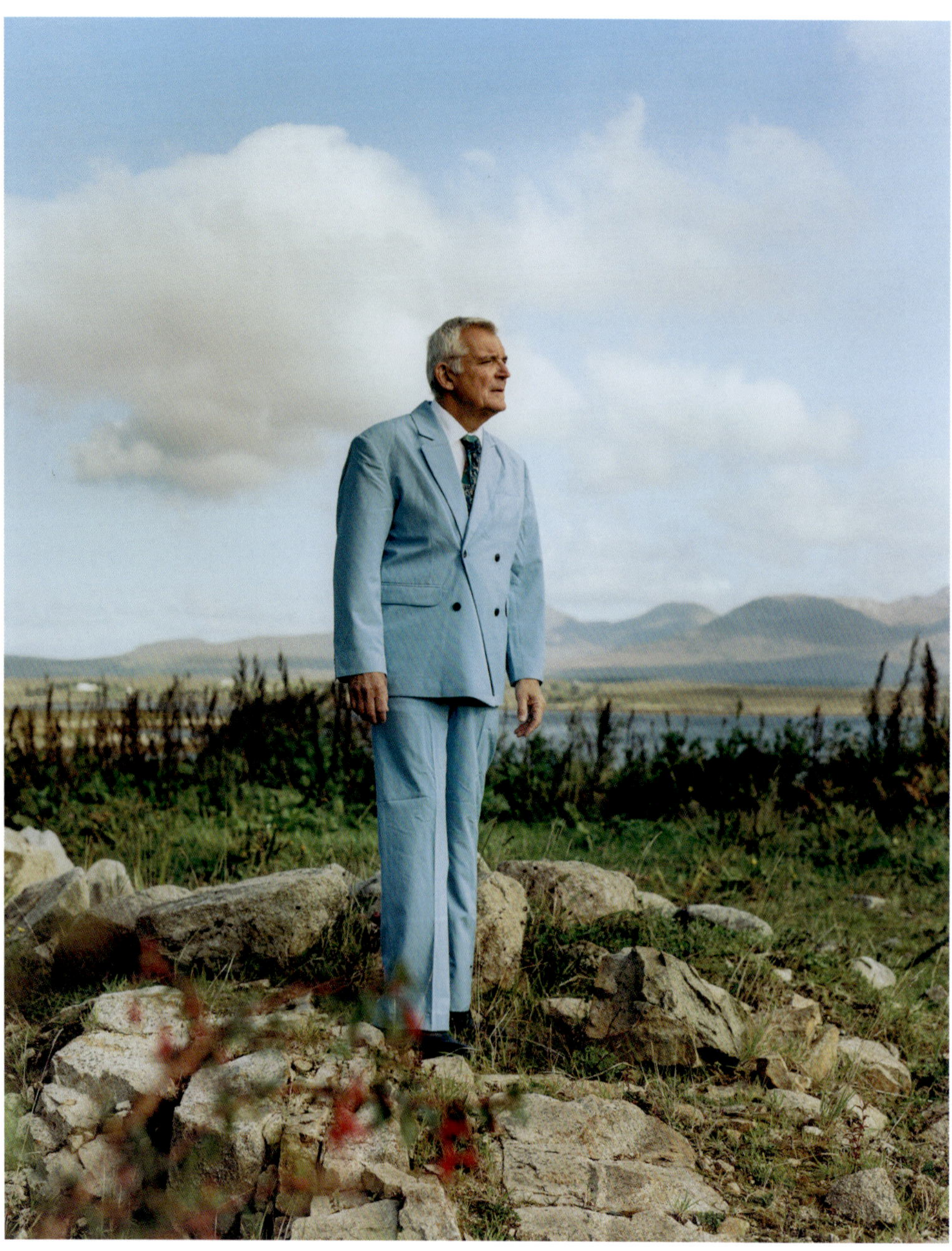

Madeleine Waller

Aging Gracefully, 2023
From the series *I spend 150 hours alone a week*
Inkjet print

Compelled to document her 88-year-old mother Valerie at her home in Chum Creek, Australia, Madeleine Waller, who lives in London, describes her limited visits with her camera as 'intense'. 'Each time I visit I wonder if this is the last time I will see her'. The tenderness of the relationship between photographer and sitter is evident. Valerie is seemingly unaware of the camera; an afternoon nap, amongst signifiers of a long lifetime, demonstrates both habitual comfort and the vulnerability of age.

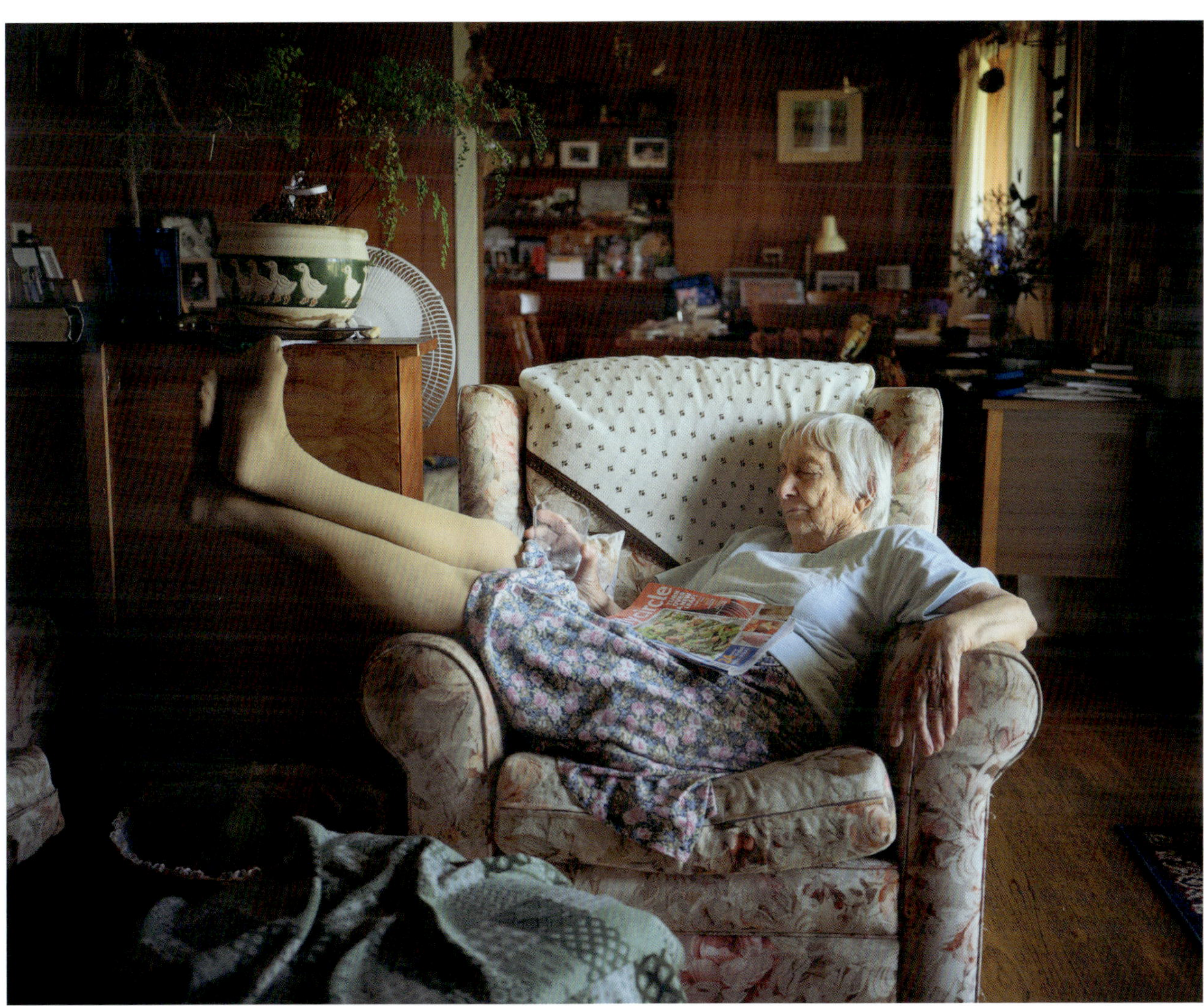

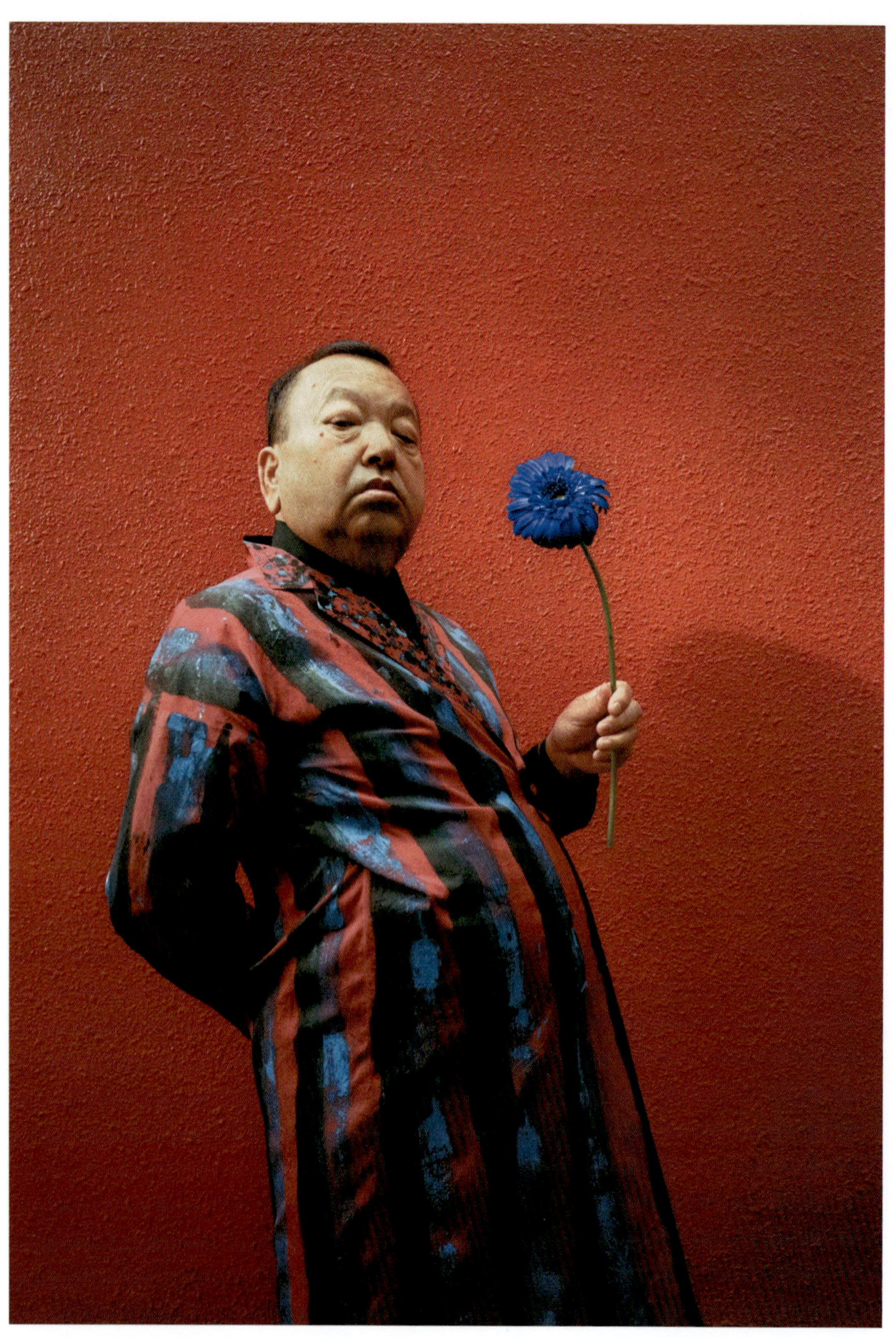

Takamasa Honda
Hiromi [Tricolor], 2023
Chromogenic print

Hiromi is a supermarket security guard in Hiroshima, Japan, here transformed in an ongoing collaboration with Takamasa Honda, who combines photography with fashion design. Influenced by the colours and forms of Henri Matisse, Honda designed and dyed kimono silk cloth and made a coat which he then hand painted. The dyed gerbera completes the constructed portrait of Hiromi – an ordinary man with 'unusual beauty' whose demeanour and stance clinches the satisfying composition.

Charlotte Hadden

Izzy, 2023
From the series *Between*
Inkjet print

This portrait of Izzy forms part of a project that Charlotte Hadden has been working on for the past seven years, portraying young transgender people in the United Kingdom. Hadden spent the afternoon with Izzy in Lincoln, photographing and getting to know her across several hours. This was the last setup of the day and, on the request of Izzy, featured her pet rat. Hadden's elegant portrait and fashion interest is evident through Izzy's coming of age composure, which balances sensitivity and self-awareness.

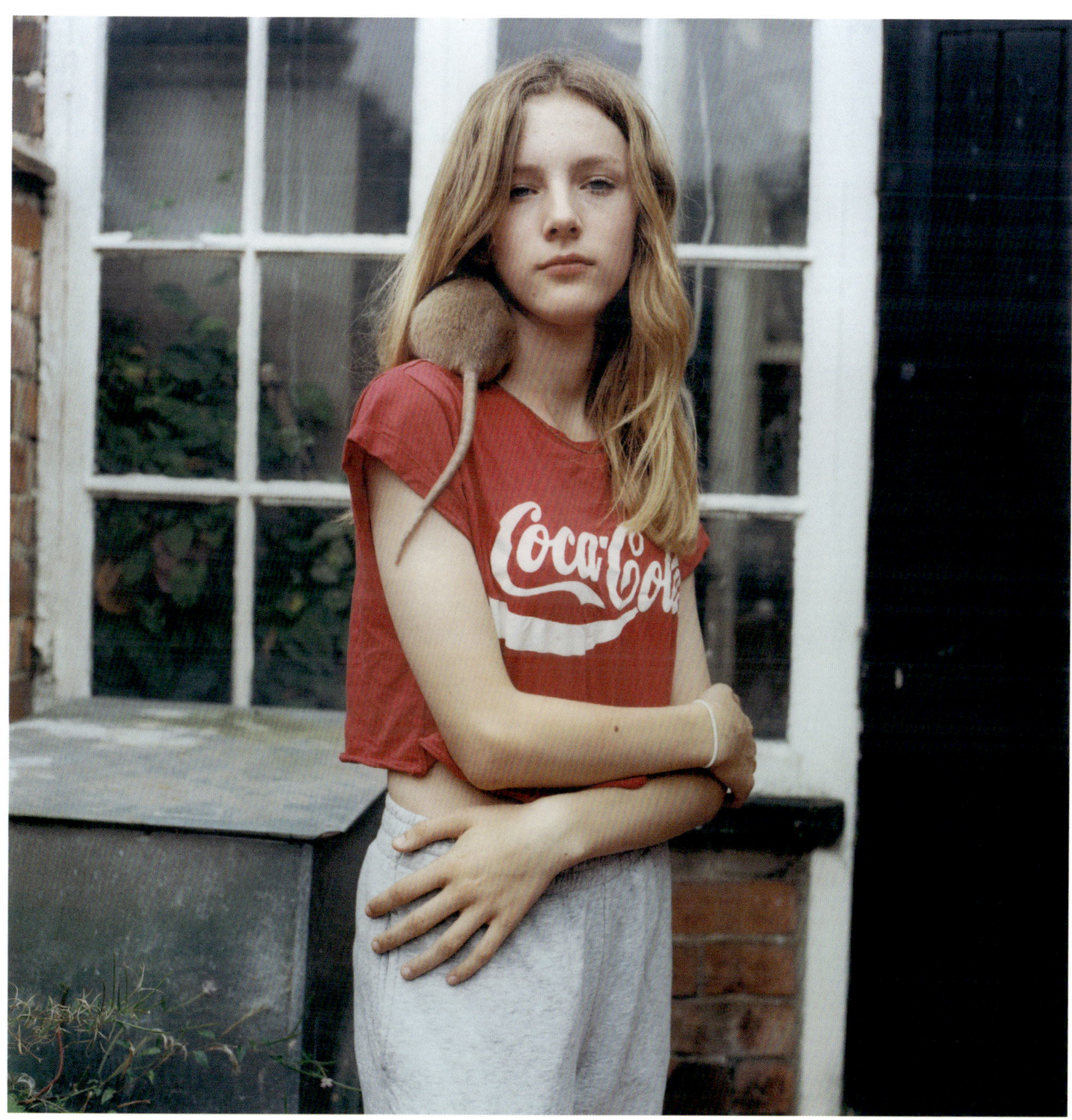

Charlotte Hadden

Mayita Mendez
Tree creature, 2023
From the series *Yo soy de aqui, I am from here*
Inkjet print

Both Mayita Mendez and her friend Kristjanne live on the sparsely populated Protection Island, Nanaimo, Canada, where this photograph was made. Kristjanne had just recorded her punk music album 'KMVP Goes Ribbit', where she sat by the local pond to record the frogs singing, basing her music on their sounds. Kristjanne asked Mendez to make an image for her album cover, 'inspired by the promise of the morning light and surrounded by the rare Garry Oak and Cedar trees'. Kristjanne lay down as if becoming a 'tree creature' in this magical moment; her handwritten tattoo 'RIBIT' just visible.

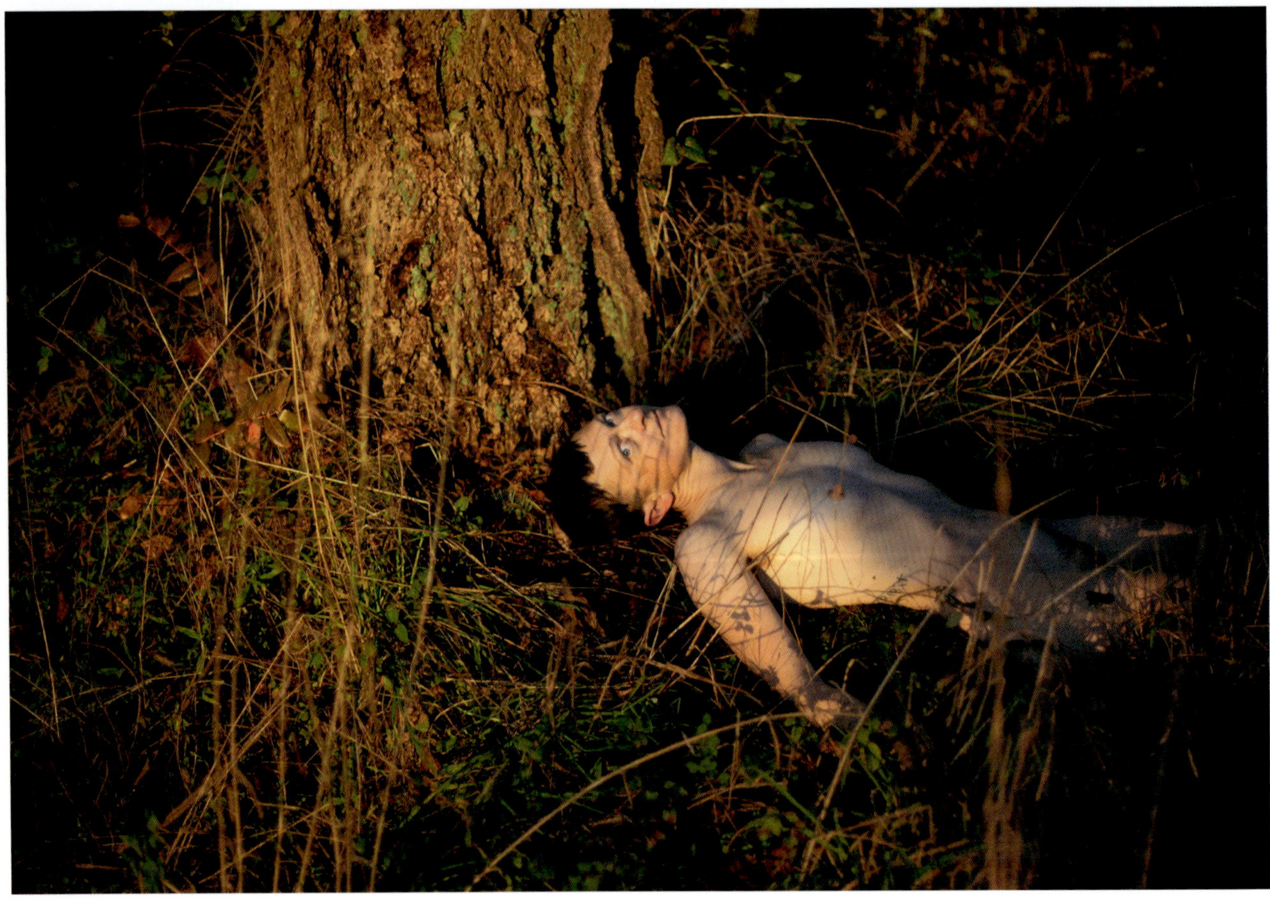

Shen Wei

Two Painters, 2023
From the series *Self-portrait*
Chromogenic print

The three figures within this photograph, made in a
Parisian studio, each speak to Shen Wei's intentions of
'capturing the essence of our conversation about art,
queerness, and self-reflection.' Shen Wei is foregrounded,
palette in hand, pose mirrored by their friend whose face
has been represented and replaced with Wei's. The final
figure is mounted on the wall; a thin sliver is visible of
the body and encourages a reading of the image which
moves beyond the physical and speaks to the varied
visible and invisible layers of an individual's identity.

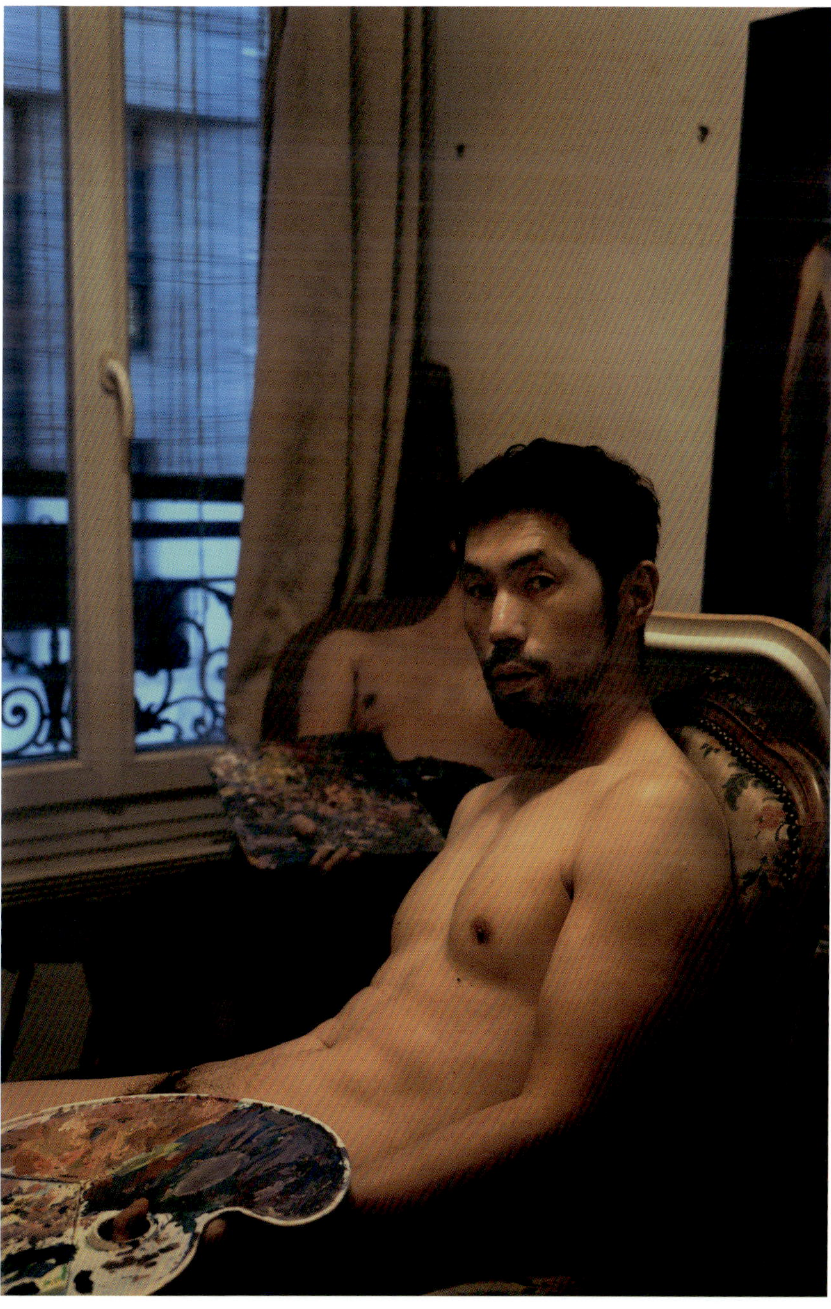

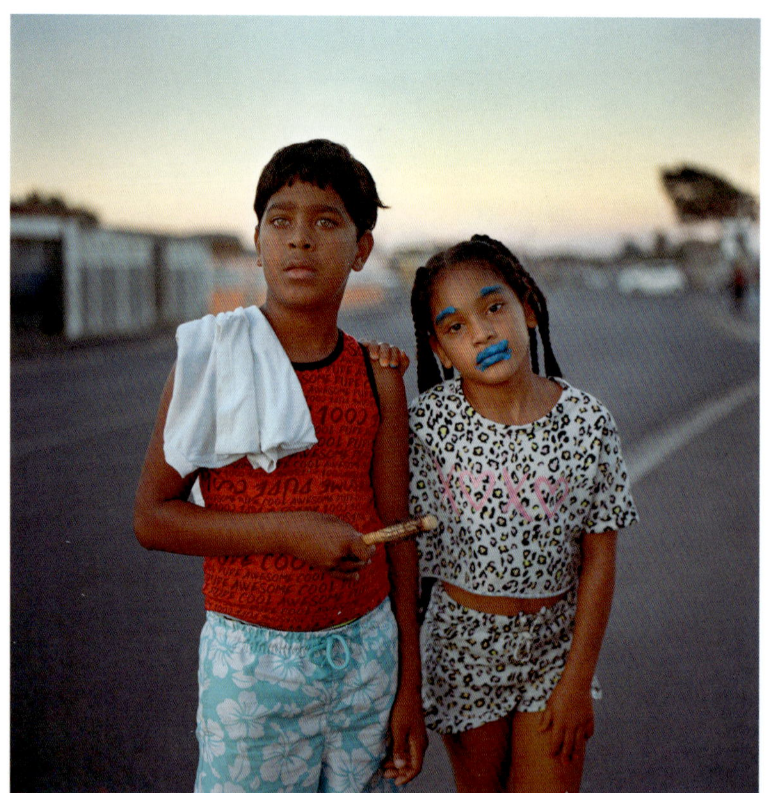

Laura Pannack

Project Hope, 2023
Project Hope, 2023
From the series *The journey home from school*
Inkjet print (above); chromogenic print (below)

Laura Pannack's series, *The journey home from school*, follows young people living in the gang governed Cape Flats area of Cape Town, South Africa, where intense street violence means they cannot play outside or walk to school. 'Together, we walk to and home from school, avoiding the daily threat of gang crossfire.' Bright blue 'makeup' and a hairbrush in one portrait suggests two friends at play, although at odds with their serious expressions. The pattern of looking, in both works, draws our gaze in and directs it out beyond the frame: a reminder of the unsafe space that surrounds. In 2014, Pannack was the recipient of the John Kobal New Work Award, generated by the Photo Portrait Prize.

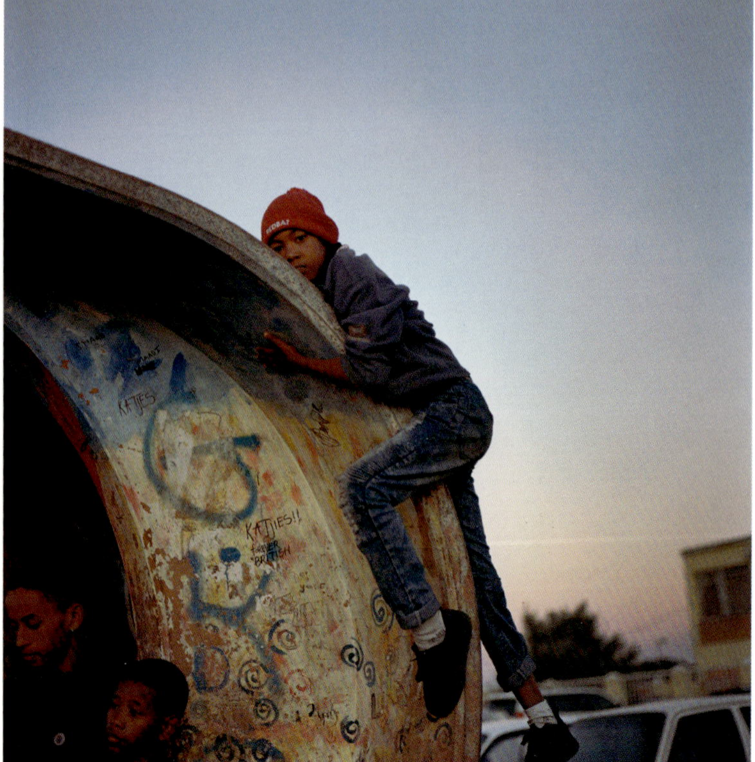

Frankie Mills

Kitchen Embrace, 2023
From the series *Good Evening,
We Are From Ukraine*
Chromogenic print

Frankie Mills captures a tender moment between Polina and her daughter, Olena, their dog Asia peeking through. On the kitchen wall, a collage of snapshots hints at the sponsors who have been hosting them since they fled Russia's invasion of Ukraine. Over two years, Mills followed the stories of Ukrainian refugees living with host families in rural Devon, England. Focusing on how communities find solutions to the uncertainty of displacement, the series aims to 'inspire others to open their doors to more people from around the world'.

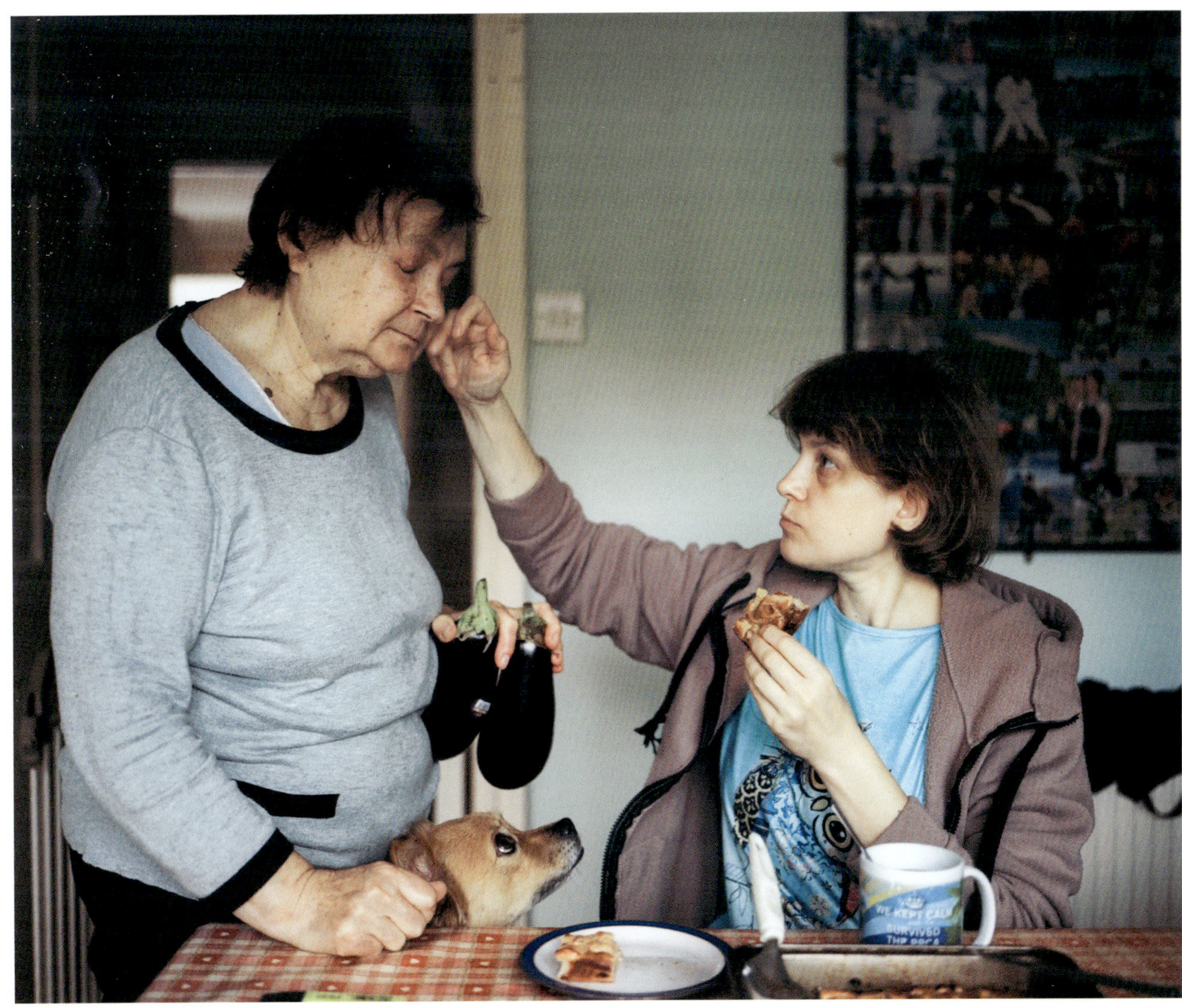

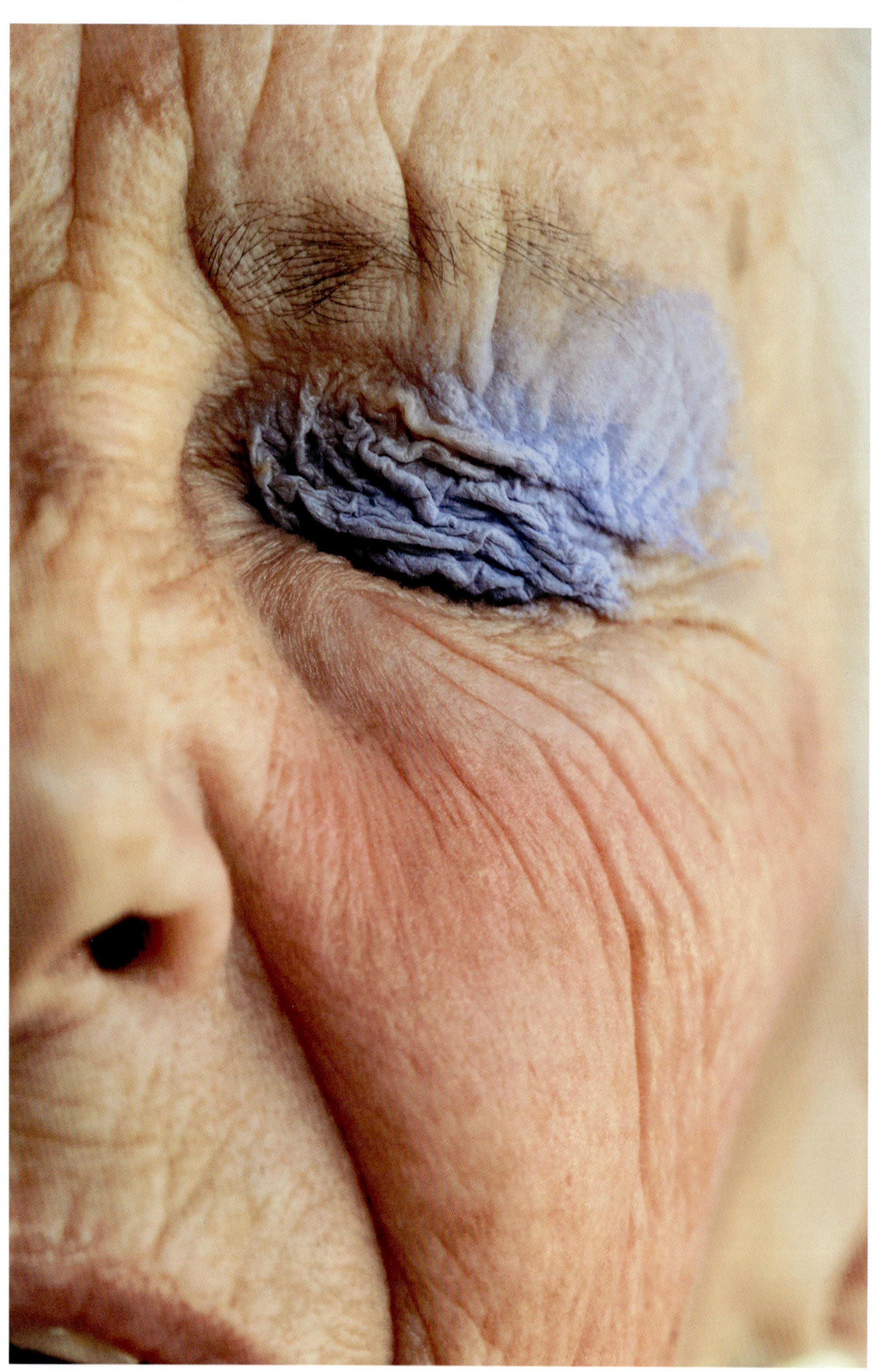

Claire Brand
Bridget, 2023
Chromogenic print

Bridget's eyes are closed so tightly that the wrinkles and contours of her face are even more deeply engrained in this closely framed photograph. The blue eyeshadow trails off beyond the eyelid and finds itself amidst the brow. Claire Brand has expressed a desire to find joy and beauty in the skin of older models, and to celebrate the lines and signs of ageing despite society's intent on avoiding the evidence of passing time.

Sandra Nagel

Phebe, 2023
From the series *I see, you see*
Chromogenic print

Sandra Nagel speaks of the connection they and their friend Phebe felt on finding this pastel pink apartment. Phebe's sleek hair, and barely there eyebrows and lashes, elevate this domestic space into a timeless, stylish fashion photograph. The expansion of fashion photography has extended ways of seeing through an appreciation of beauty in all of its forms; a conversation that Nagel's image contributes to.

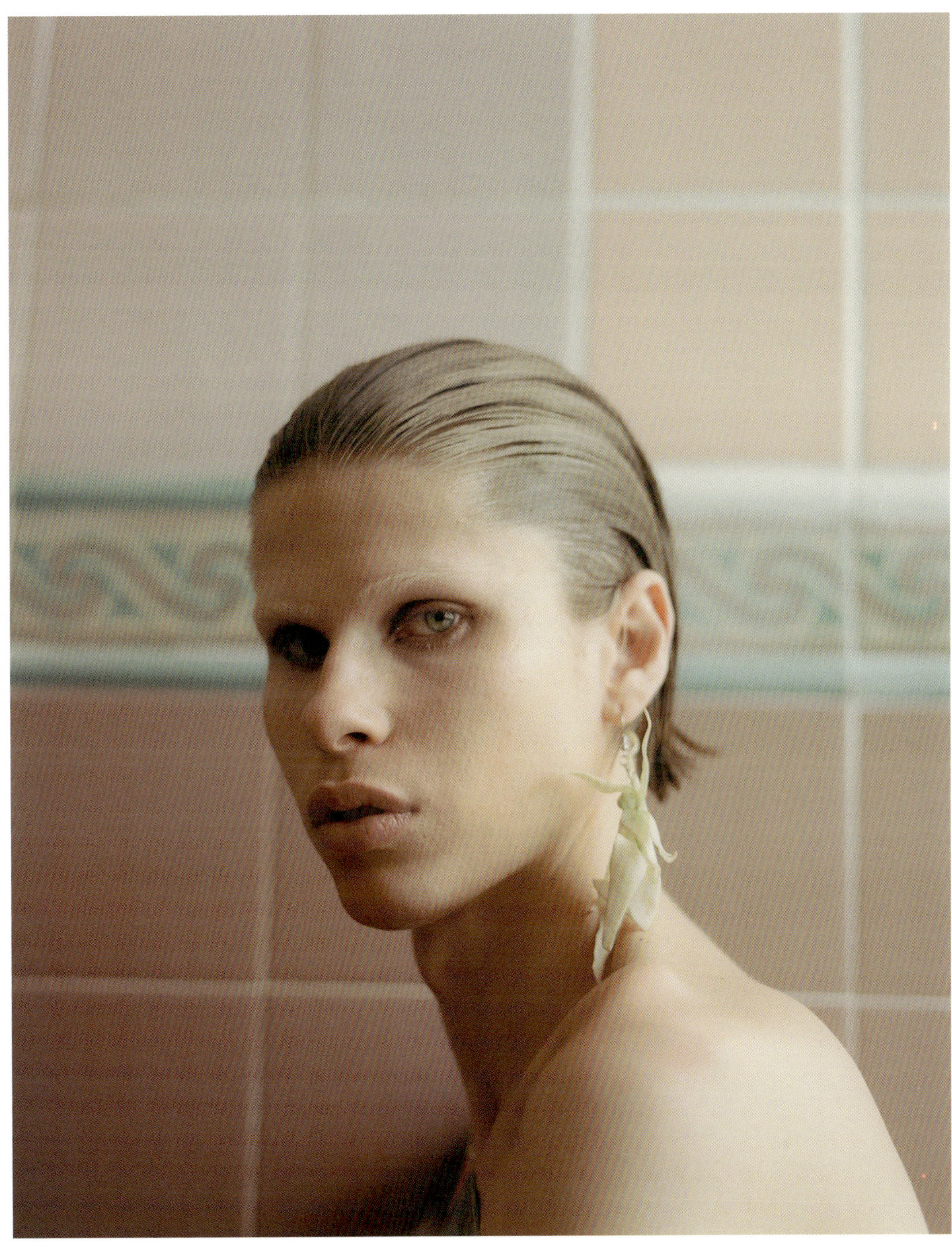

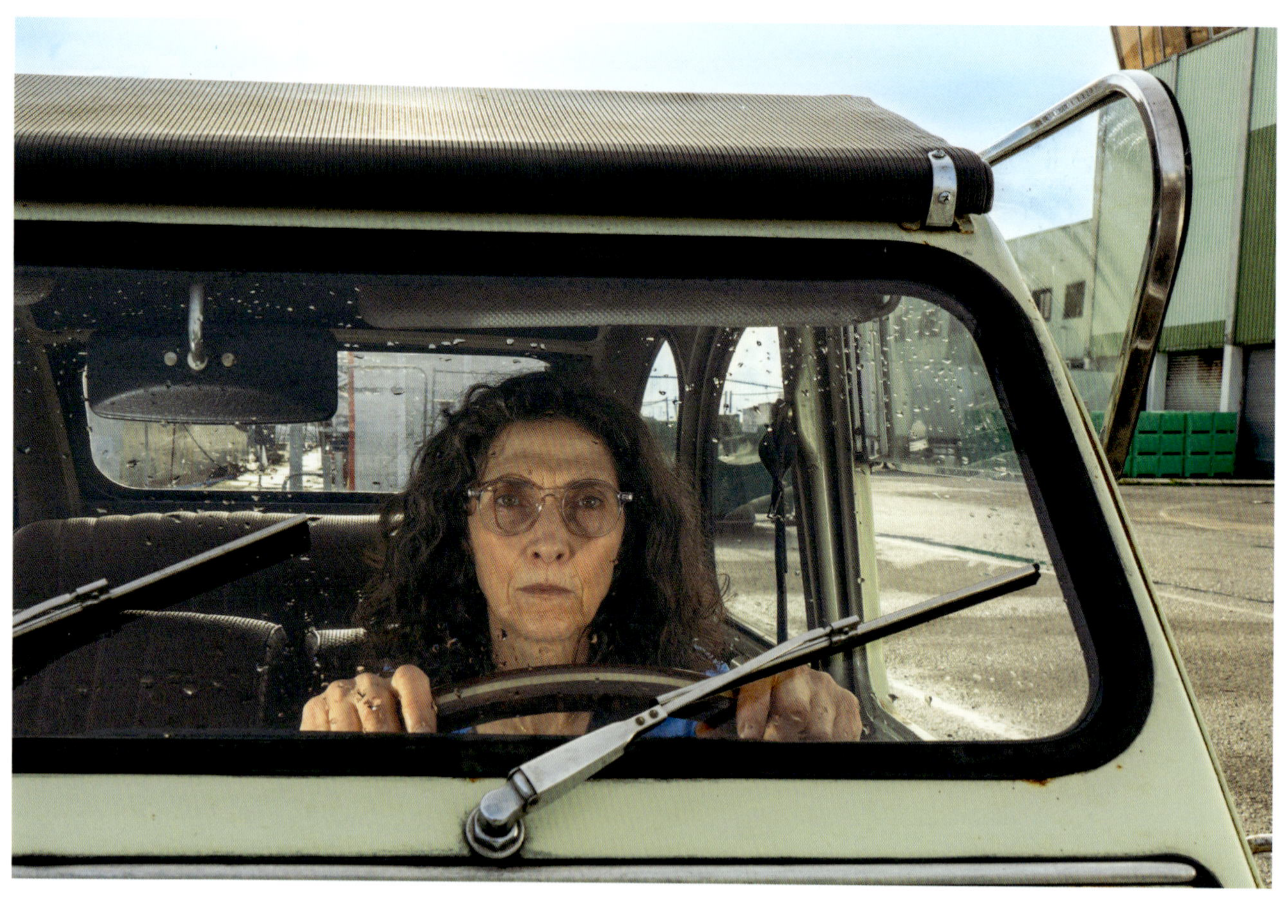

Mathilde Vieilledent
Car, 2023
From the series *Relou*
Inkjet print

Gripping the steering wheel, Mathilde Vieilledent's mother Odile stares out through the rain-splattered windshield of a vintage car. Behind this cinematic portrait is a serious message about the burden of street harassment on women in France. It forms part of the series *Relou* – meaning both 'heavy' and 'annoying' in French verlan slang – in which the photographer restages techniques used by victims to avoid harassment; here, choosing to drive rather than walking alone.

Farren van Wyk

Boycott Outspan Blood Oranges, 2023
From the series *Mixedness is my Mythology*
Inkjet print

Holding our gaze, Farren van Wyk crushes a blood orange in her fist. In a self-portrait ripe with symbolism, this gesture addresses the graphic imagery of a 1970s Dutch boycott campaign against South African Apartheid, while the carefully arranged fruit evokes the traditions of still life painting in the Netherlands. In her ongoing series, the photographer draws upon her South African and Dutch heritage to interrogate the complex legacies of colonialism and Apartheid. Van Wyk's work is often in collaboration with her family. Her younger brother Alexander collaborated on this portrait.

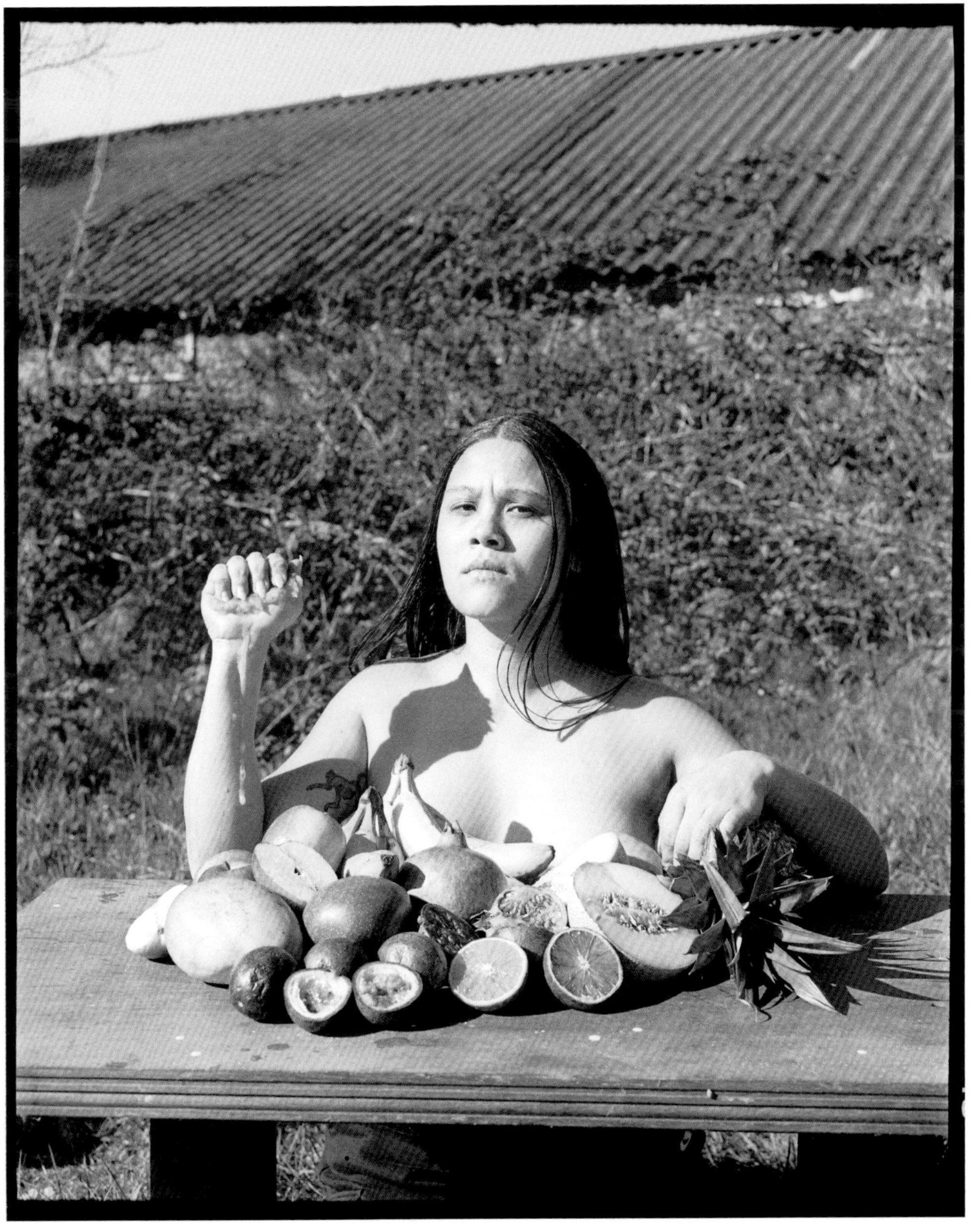

Ville Niiranen

Family Portrait, 2023
From the series *The Admirable Fabric of Masculine Intelligence*
Chromogenic print

In this alternative family portrait, Niiranen lines up in goal alongside his wife, Nicole, and daughters, Laura and Maija. Taken in the Swiss mountain village where the family spend their holidays, the photoshoot began with a series of improvised scenes around football, with each member taking a different role. This playful and collaborative approach informs Niiranen's autobiographical series *The Admirable Fabric of Masculine Intelligence*, in which the photographer examines gender roles from his perspective as a stay at home dad.

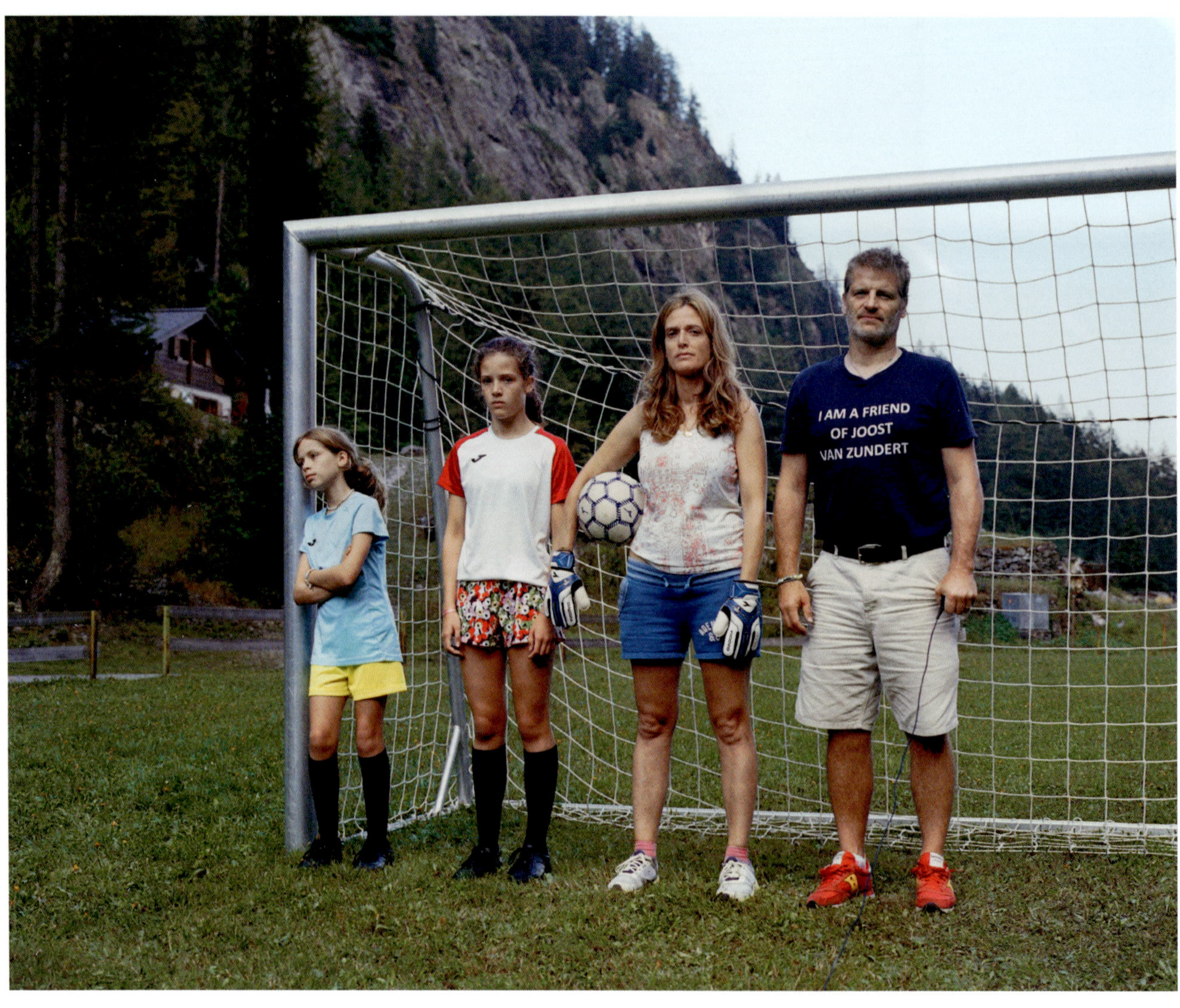

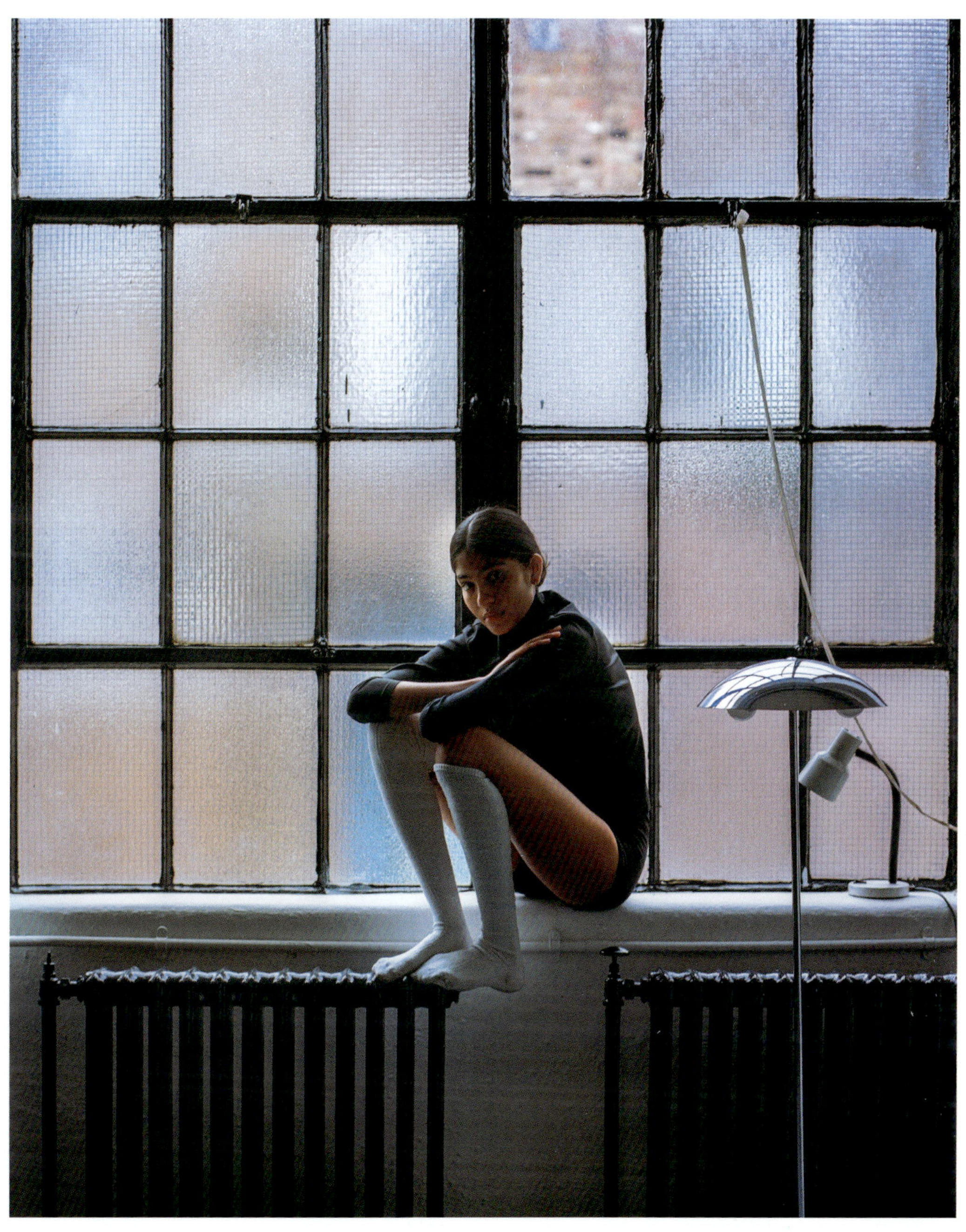

Jiayue Jenny Li
Off-duty, 2024
Chromogenic print

Graphic design graduate, Jiayue Jenny Li, portrays her childhood friend from South Africa, Antara, in between clothing changes on a fashion shoot – her aim to document the tedious, unglamorous side of modelling. The geometry of the windows at Outsourced Spaces – a studio and vintage clothing store, where styling and shooting can coexist – dwarfs the sitter, who appears vulnerable in scale but assured in gaze. Using a Mamiya medium format camera for the first time, Li hand-printed, scanned and retouched the image before making the final print.

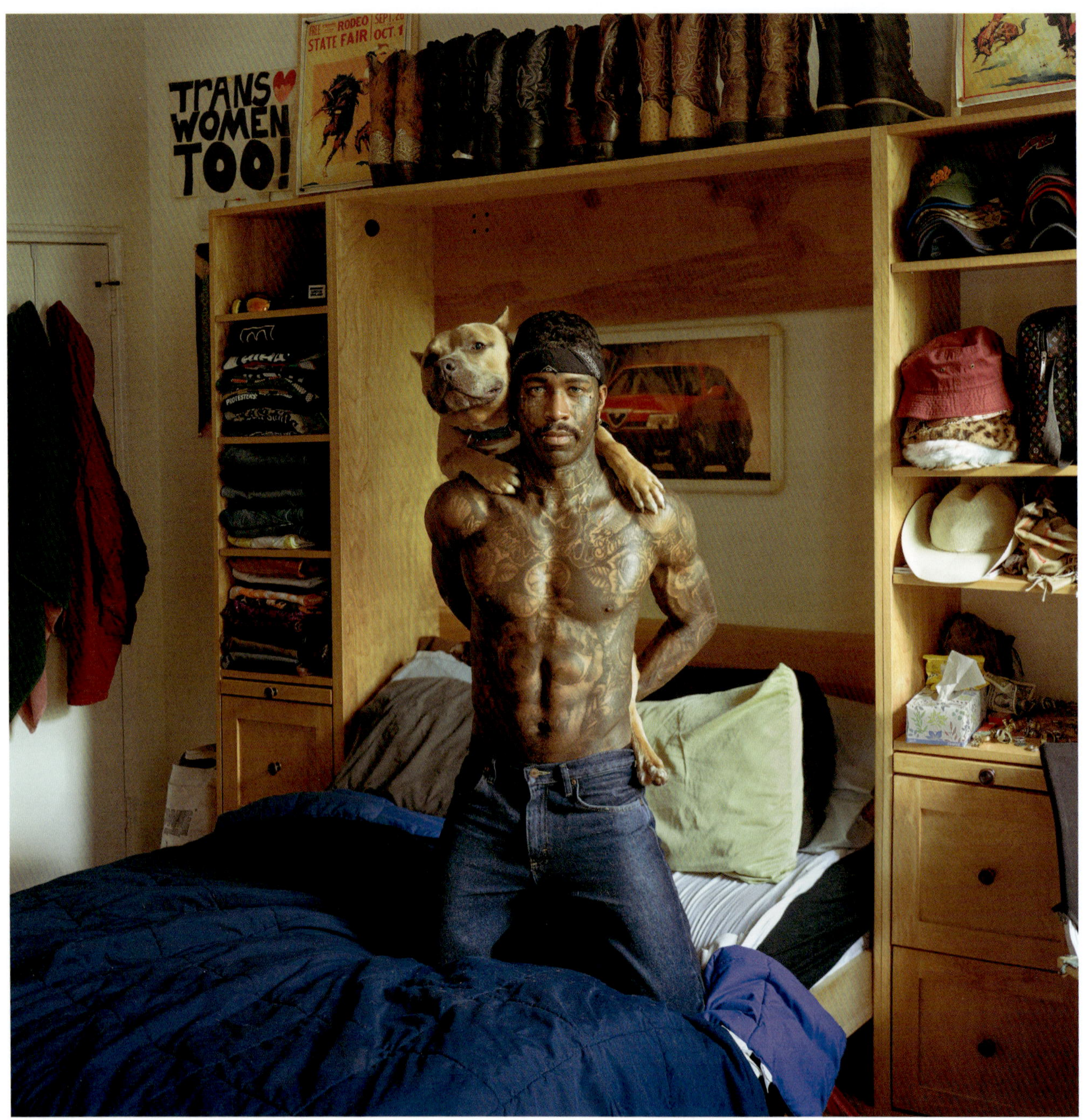

Stas Ginzburg
Yves & Banjo, 2024
From the series *Sanctuary*
Inkjet print

Stas Ginzburg's photo series, *Sanctuary*, documents queer and trans folx in their homes. Through the images, we are invited into people's personal spaces of comfort and rest. Yves and Banjo pose against a scene of stacked hats, a row of cowboy boots, and a number of posters, ranging from cars to protest signs. Ginzburg's ambitions are clear, with the series 'highlighting how the environments and objects within these spaces contribute to their unique narratives and experiences'.

Laurie Broughton

Nelly aka Queen Niche, 2024
From the series *The Welsh Voice*
Chromogenic print

This arresting portrait of Nelly (Queen Niche) forms part of a series portraying Welsh women who are human rights and peace activists, made in collaboration with Emily Hawkins. Laurie Broughton met Nelly while attending weeks of Palestine solidarity demonstrations in Cardiff, building a relationship before asking them to sit for a portrait. The simple fabric backdrop foregrounds Nelly's direct gaze and defiant pose, emphasising her role as a community leader. For Broughton, activists like Nelly 'fit seamlessly into a long, resilient tradition of tirelessly supporting everyone in Wales to play their role as global citizens.'

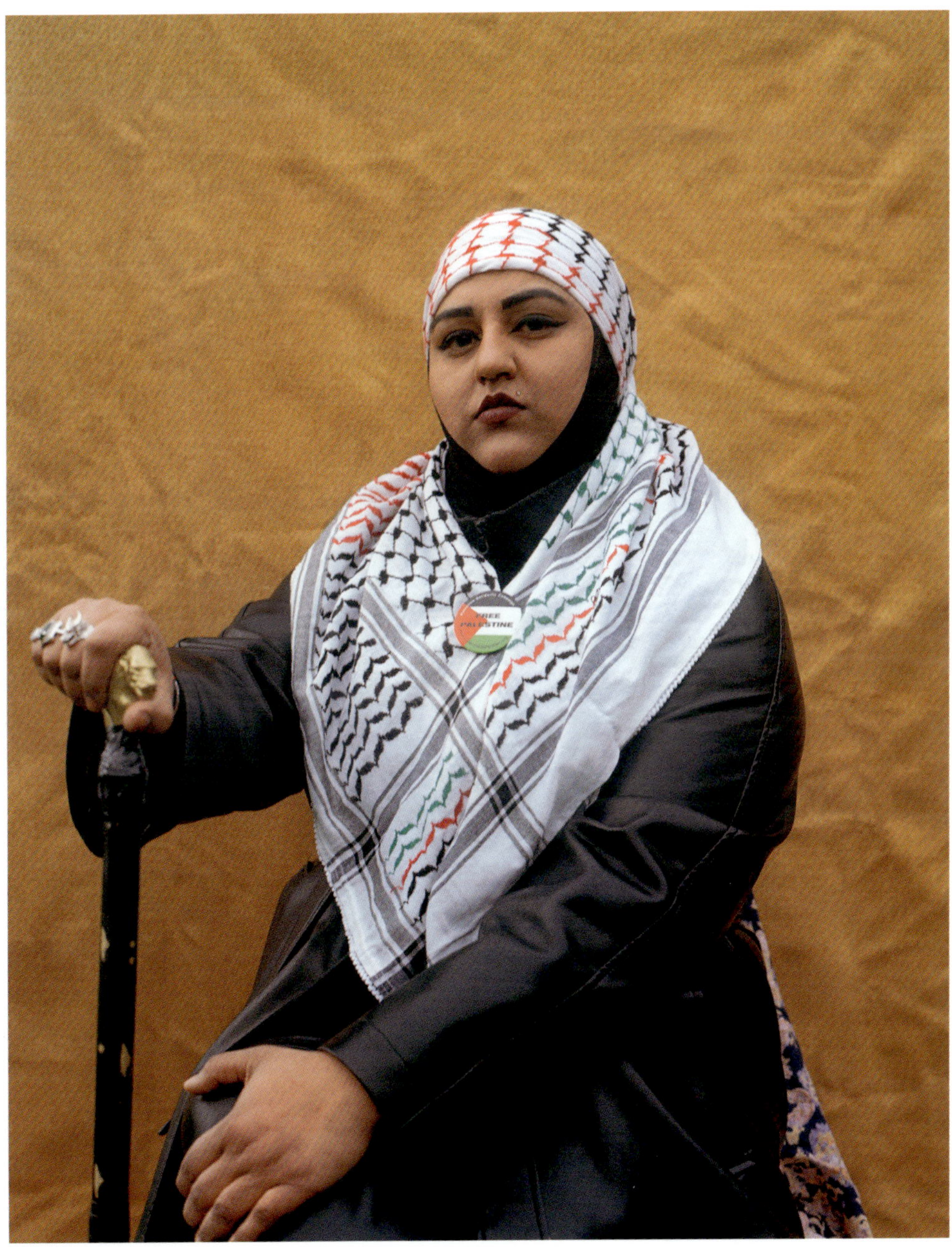

Juanita Richards
Surf Girls Jamaica, 2024
From the series *Surf Sisterhood JA*
Chromogenic print

Juanita Richards was photographing the Surf Girls of Jamaica, a collective run by Afro-Caribbean surf pioneer Imani Wilma, the day she encountered Nya Tafari and Megumi sprawled on a surfboard, playfully shielding their eyes from the sun with pebbles. The relaxed nature of the portrait is amplified by the camera angle – the sea's edge just clipped by the frame. Director and photographer, Richards found 'safety, sisterhood and serenity' among this organisation, based just 10 minutes from the bustle of Kingston. The ethos of empowerment for these young women through the sport is echoed by Richards's own inclusive practice, where she seeks to represent a positive diversity of cultures.

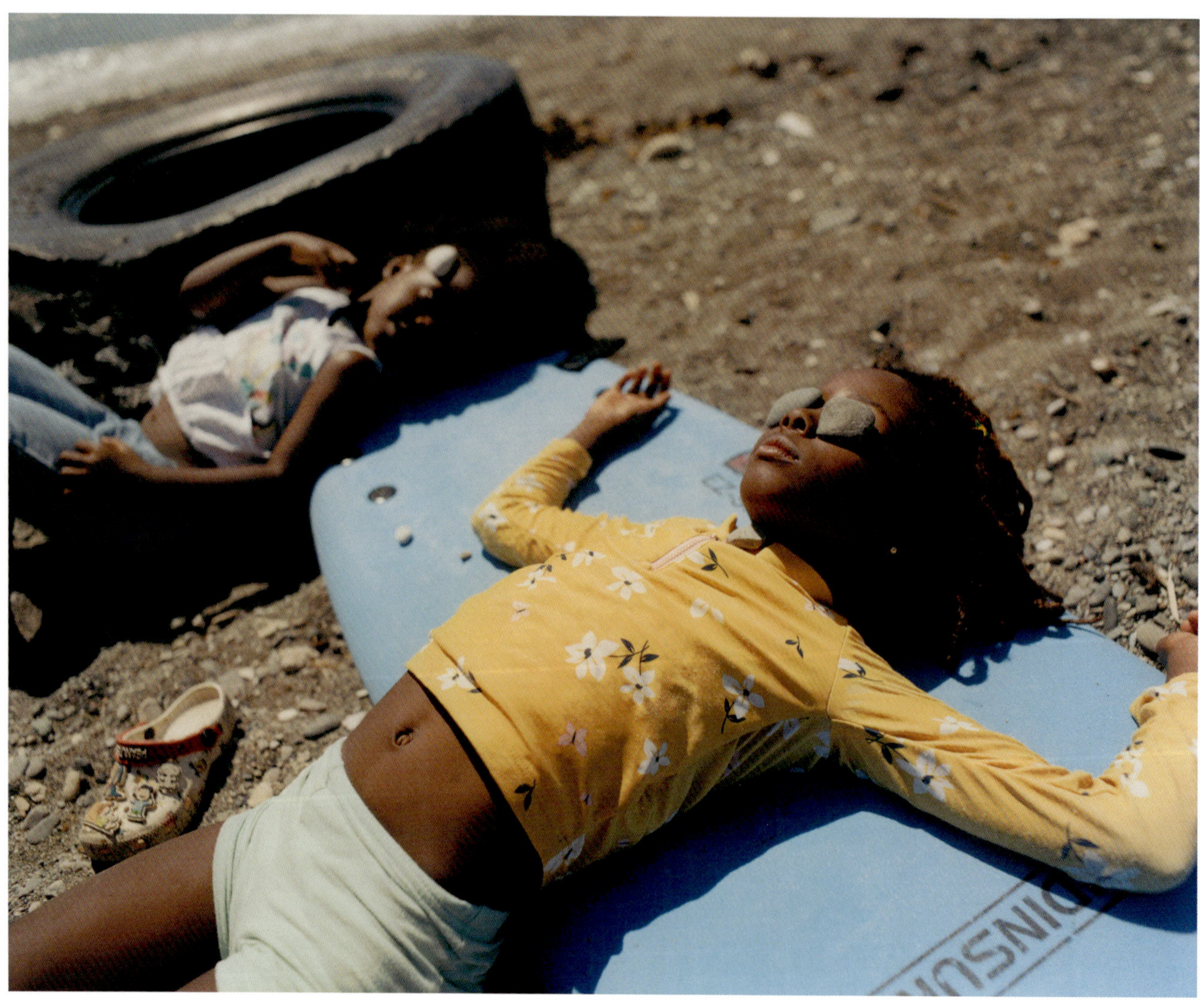

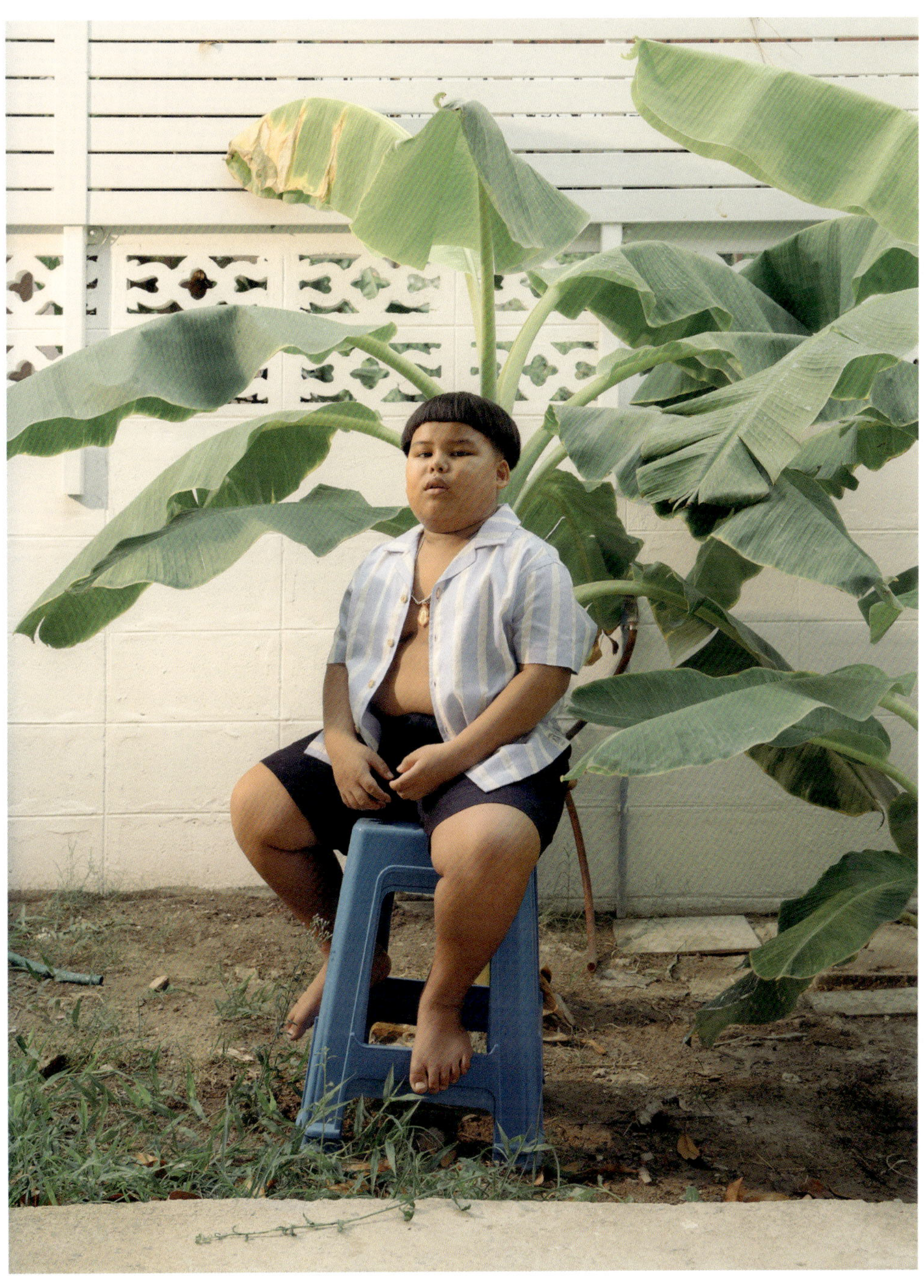

Patarit Pinyopiphat

Soi32, 2024
From the series *Soi32 / 3PM*
Chromogenic print

Patarit Pinyopiphat is a Nonthaburi, Thailand, born and based photographer. He uses *soi*, a side street, as the location and name for his series, generated by years of walking and observing his neighbourhood's ambience throughout the day, 'to me, around 3pm is the best, it generates the best light.' Ar-po is a child actor whose strength of character and ease in front of the camera leads his gaze to meet ours; his sharp haircut echoing the pattern created by the arching banana leaves.

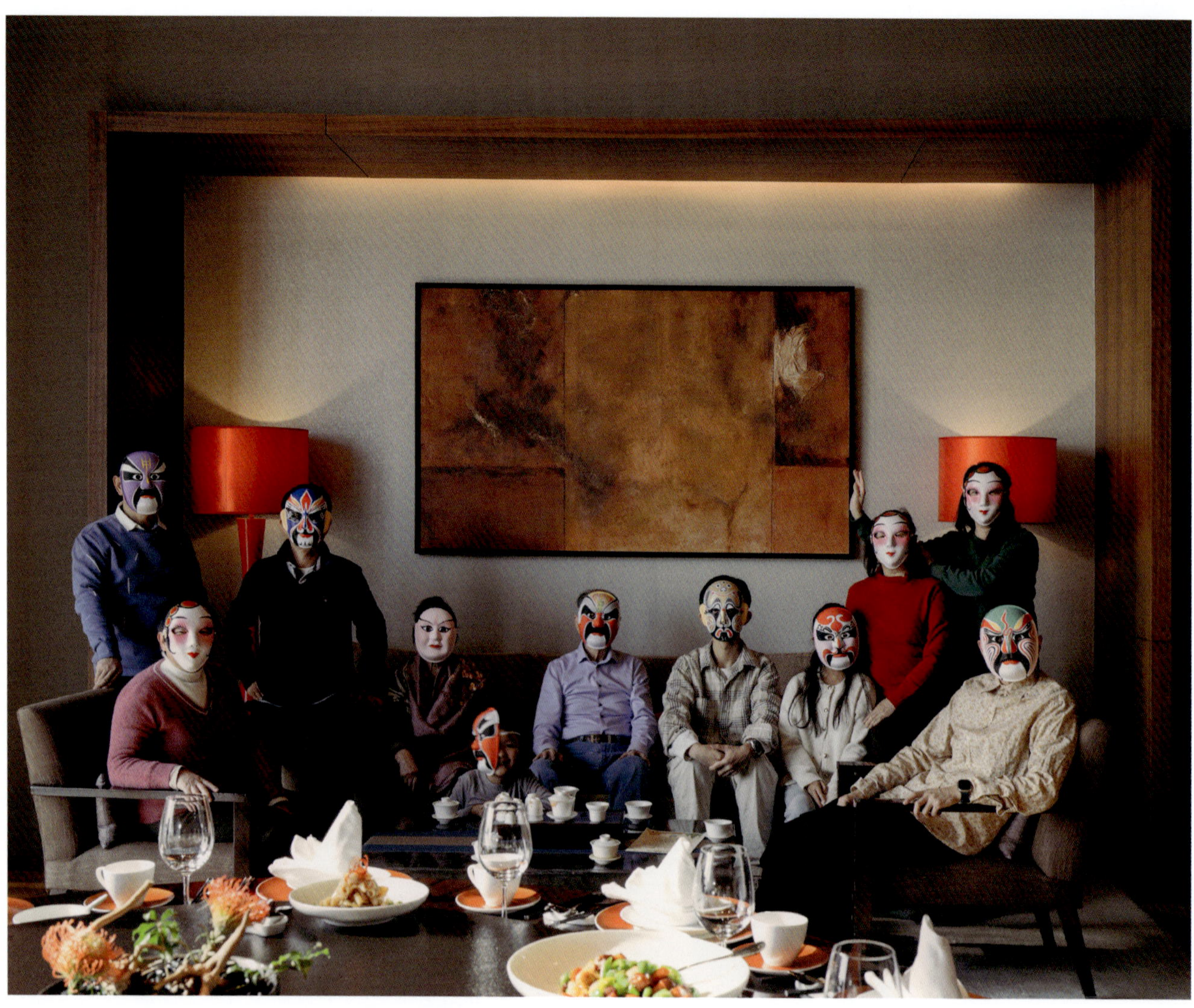

Kun Song

Untitled #1, 2023
From the series *Ju "剧" (Part II)*
Inkjet print

What could have made for a traditional family portrait – several people, possibly spanning a number of generations, gathered together before a symmetrical backdrop and pleasing artwork – has been transformed into an image of performance and ambiguity. The masks are elaborate in their design and make reading the expressions and intentions difficult. The one half slipped mask reveals a large smile, introducing a clearer reality. The Chinese title of the series translates as 'drama' and explores masking and personas in social contexts.

Polly Braden

Yuliia, at 17, in Warsaw, with her grandparents, 2023
From the series *Leaving Ukraine*
Chromogenic print

Polly Braden's series *Leaving Ukraine* portrays women and girls who have been forced to leave their homes following the Russian invasion of Ukraine. It brings together photographs, personal films and conversation. Braden's portrait was exhibited at the Foundling Museum in 2024. After meeting Yuliia in Bulgaria in 2022, Braden collaborated with her for two years to tell the story of three school friends living far apart. Yuliia is depicted with her grandparents, edged out of the frame. The sense of separation is enhanced by this composition and Yuliia's averted downward gaze. 'Many of us feel overwhelmed by the loss of friends and the inability to meet them. Everyone goes online and it's very isolating.'

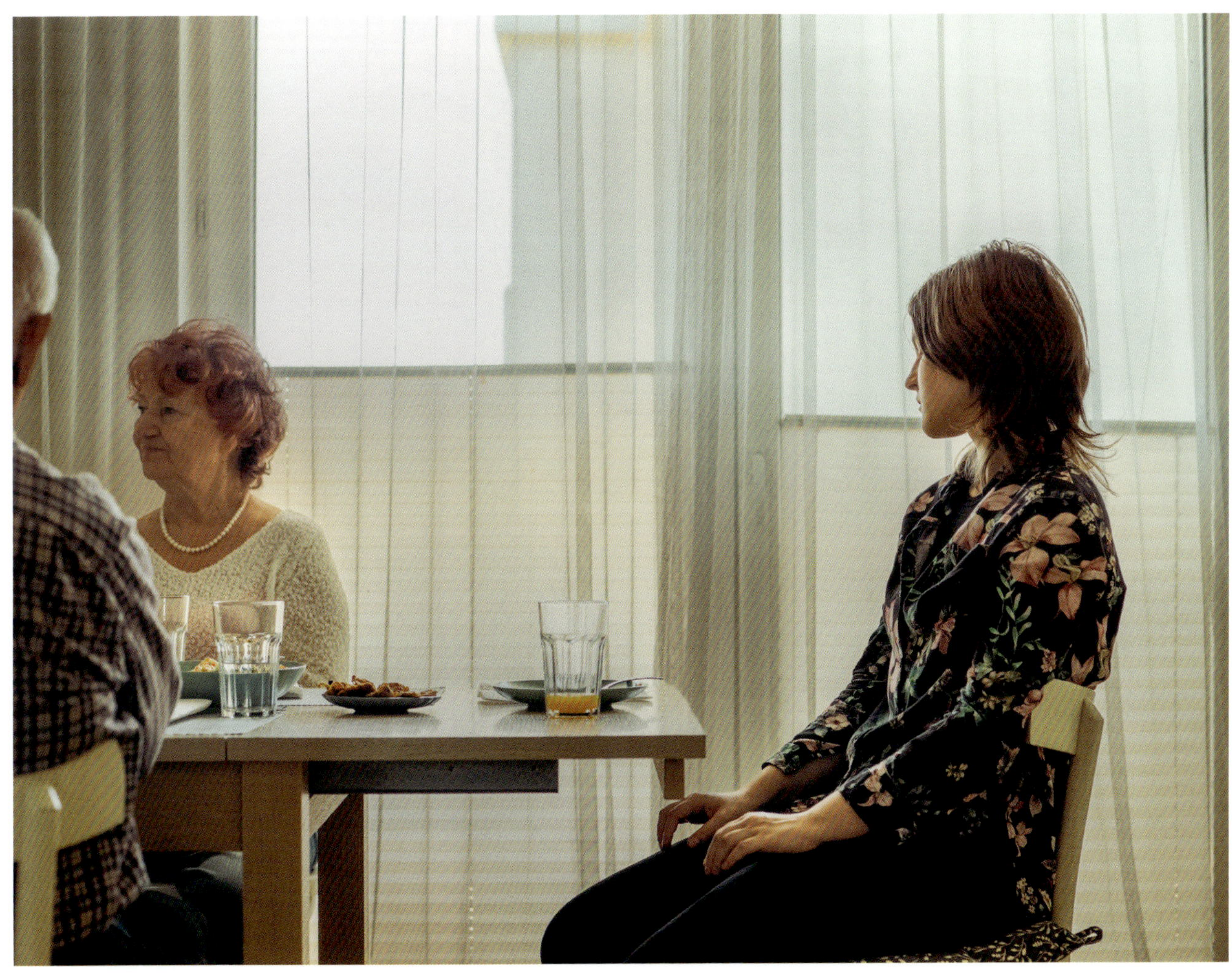

Drew Gardner

Kwesi Bowman descendant of Andrew Jackson Smith, 2023
Deanna Stanford Walz descendant of Harriet Tubman, 2023
From the series *Descendants of Black civil war combatants*
Inkjet prints after original tintypes

Drew Gardner's series brings overlooked figures of American history to light, restaging photographs of Black American civil war combatants. Gardner recreates an 1860s photograph of Harriet Tubman, American abolitionist and social activist, featuring her great-great-grandniece, Deanna. In another image, Kwesi poses as his great-great-grandfather, Andrew Jackson Smith, a soldier in the Union Army who received the highest military accolade for his service in the American civil war. The series captures likeness in a disarmingly convincing way, utilising handmade costumes and historical props, and photographed using a tintype plate camera in an authentic daylight studio.

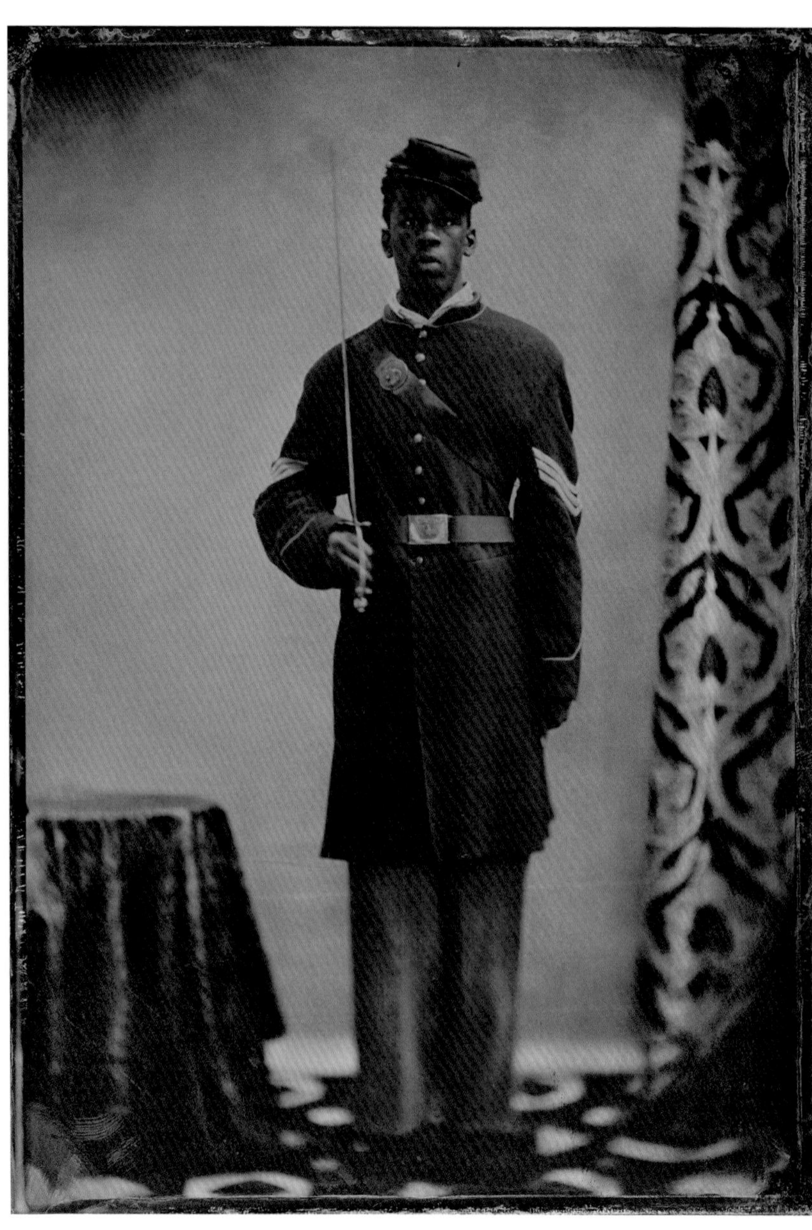

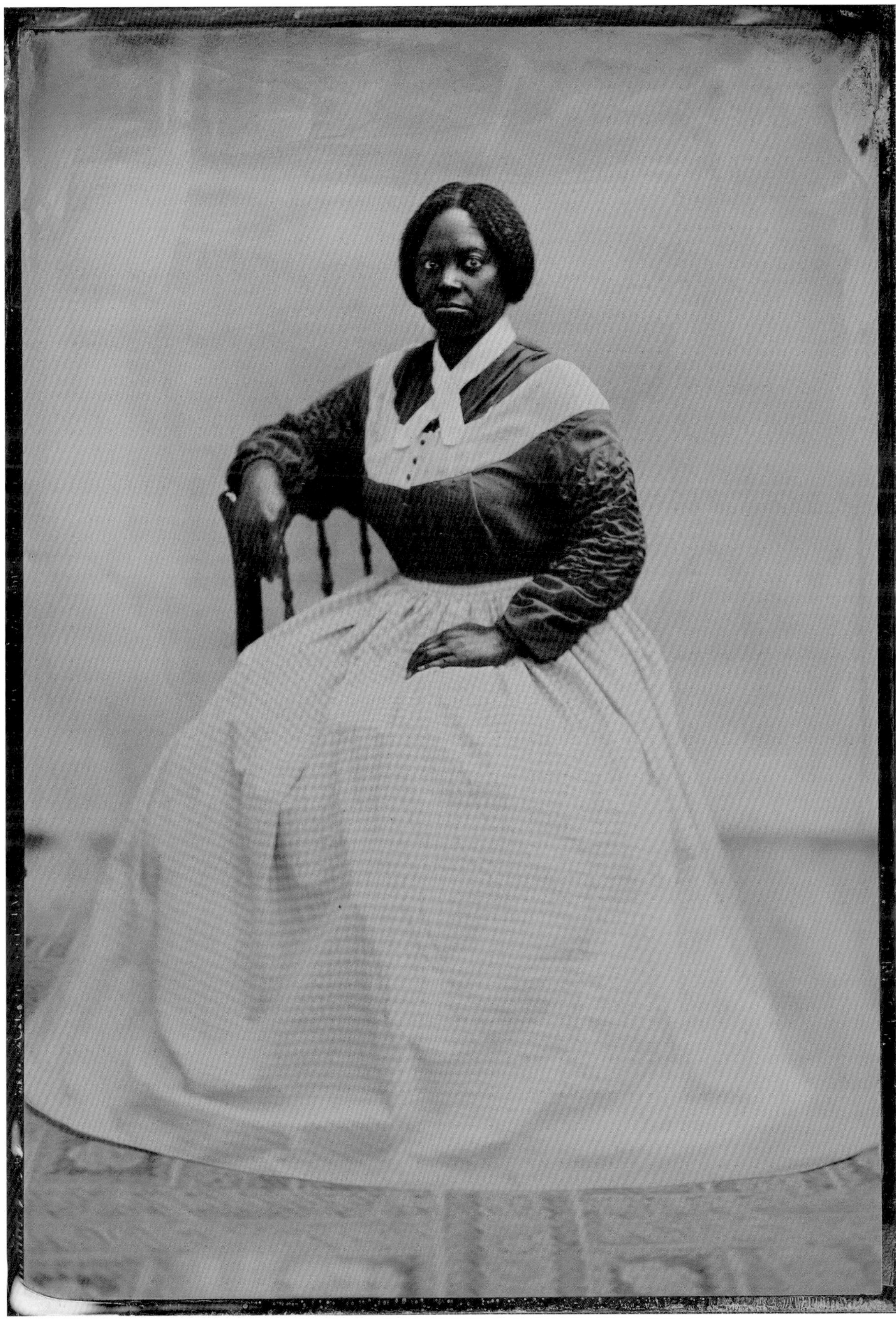

Maria Lax
Erkki, wearing his fur hat, 2024
Inkjet print

The late winter sun illuminates Erkki's home in Northern
Finland. The weather can be felt in the shadows cast by
the light and in the fur hat he wears indoors. His wife's
cross stitched version of *The Fighting Capercaillies*,
a Finnish painting by Ferdinand von Wright, hangs on
the wall to indicate a way of life soon to be eclipsed.
This portrait is one of a series of works by Maria Lax,
capturing the older generations of her family and a way
of life that is rapidly disappearing. A few months after
this photograph was taken, Erkki passed away.

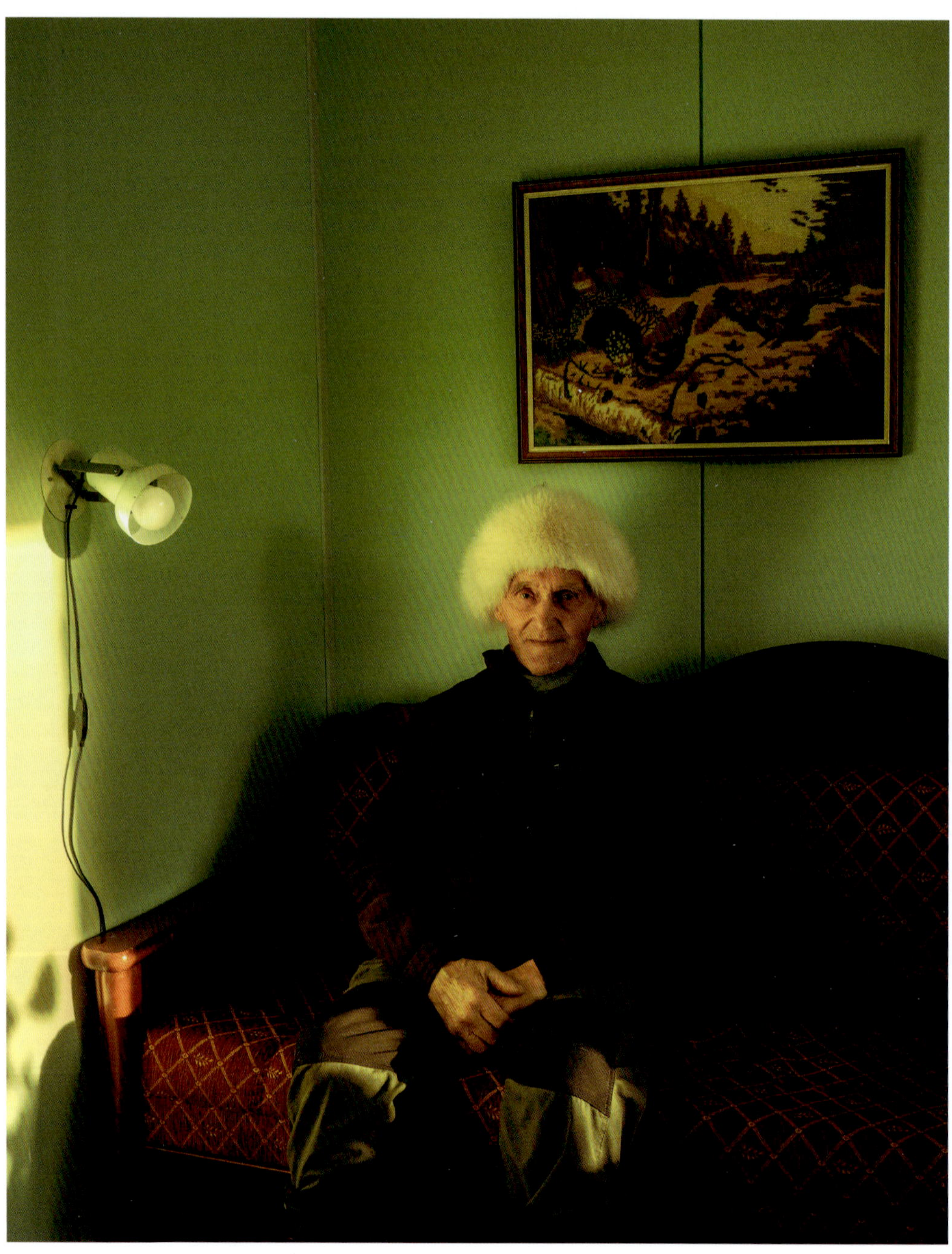

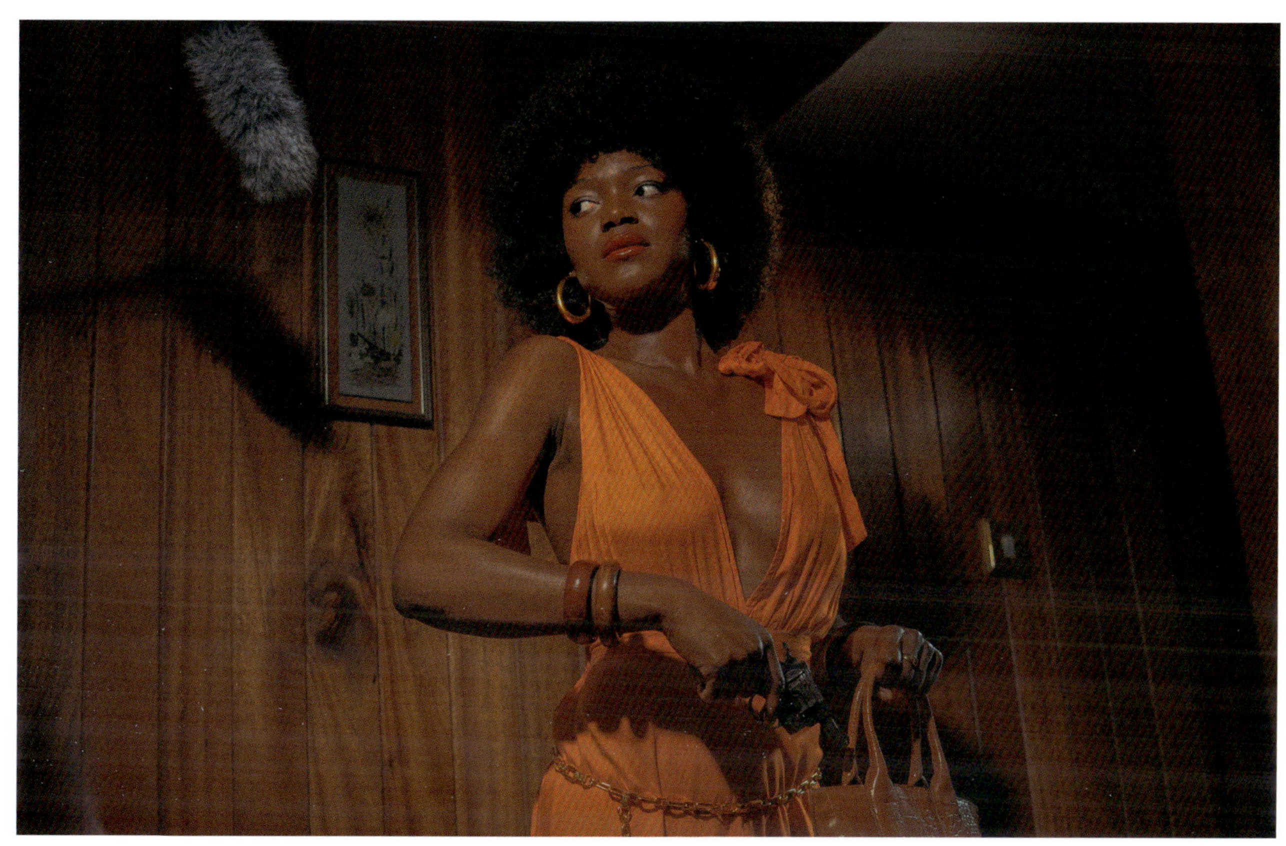

Alice Elizabeth Harris

Flore, 2024
From the series *A Study in Character*
Chromogenic print

Alice Elizabeth Harris recreates a film still aesthetic in homage to 1970s cinema. The Pam Grier inspired scene is from an ongoing series on 'the portrayal of self' and invites viewers to revel in the film and decade-specific details. The pistol and dangling mic mirror each other in their angle and shape, both seemingly ready to spring into action. The low camera angle and tight grip on Flore's handbag intensifies the feeling of action and suspense in the frame.

Kasia Wozniak

Stephen Jones, 2023
Tintype

Unusually, Kasia Wozniak combines a labour intensive historical process with a commercial proposition. This portrait was made to complement an interview featuring British milliner Stephen Jones for *10 Magazine*. Wozniak set up a darkroom in the basement of Jones's atelier in Covent Garden, London, creating nine portraits. 'Wet plate collodion has a beautiful rhythm. The plate is poured, sensitized, immediately exposed, developed, and fixed. Each step takes time, so there are few opportunities for retakes.' Through the long 20 second exposure, Wozniak creates an ethereal portrait.

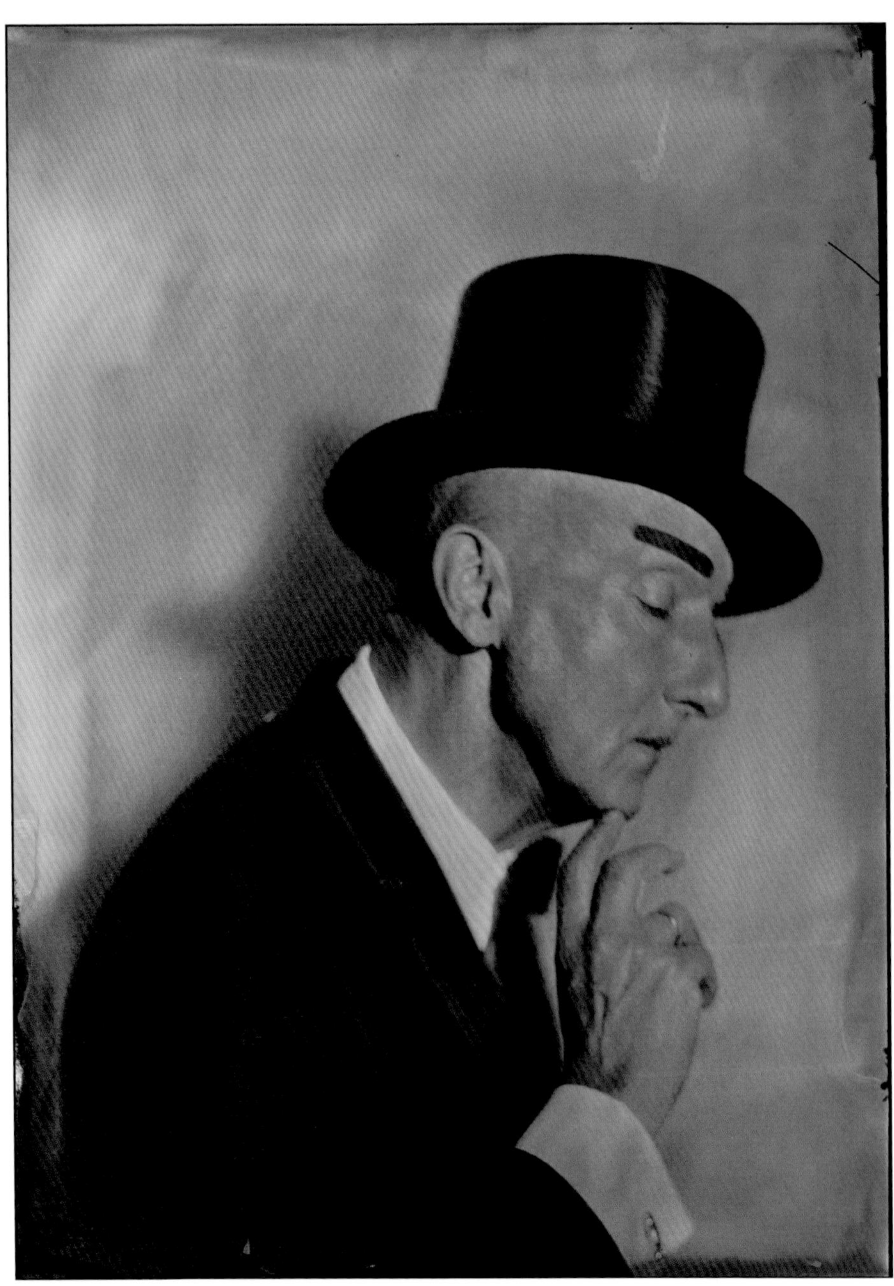

Shahid Bashir

Cold Fire, 2023
Inkjet print

Shahid Bashir photographs Adukita, his friend and model, who is represented by the modelling agency D1LON. At his home, Bashir intuitively captures an incredibly harmonious composition, punctuated by the engagement of the sitter, who is framed within a fireplace. Her gaze is unapologetic and alluringly powerful. Bashir, who has worked on inclusivity in the arts, is currently using psychology as an artistic tool to understand the 'authentic self' in relation to the fluidity of the human condition.

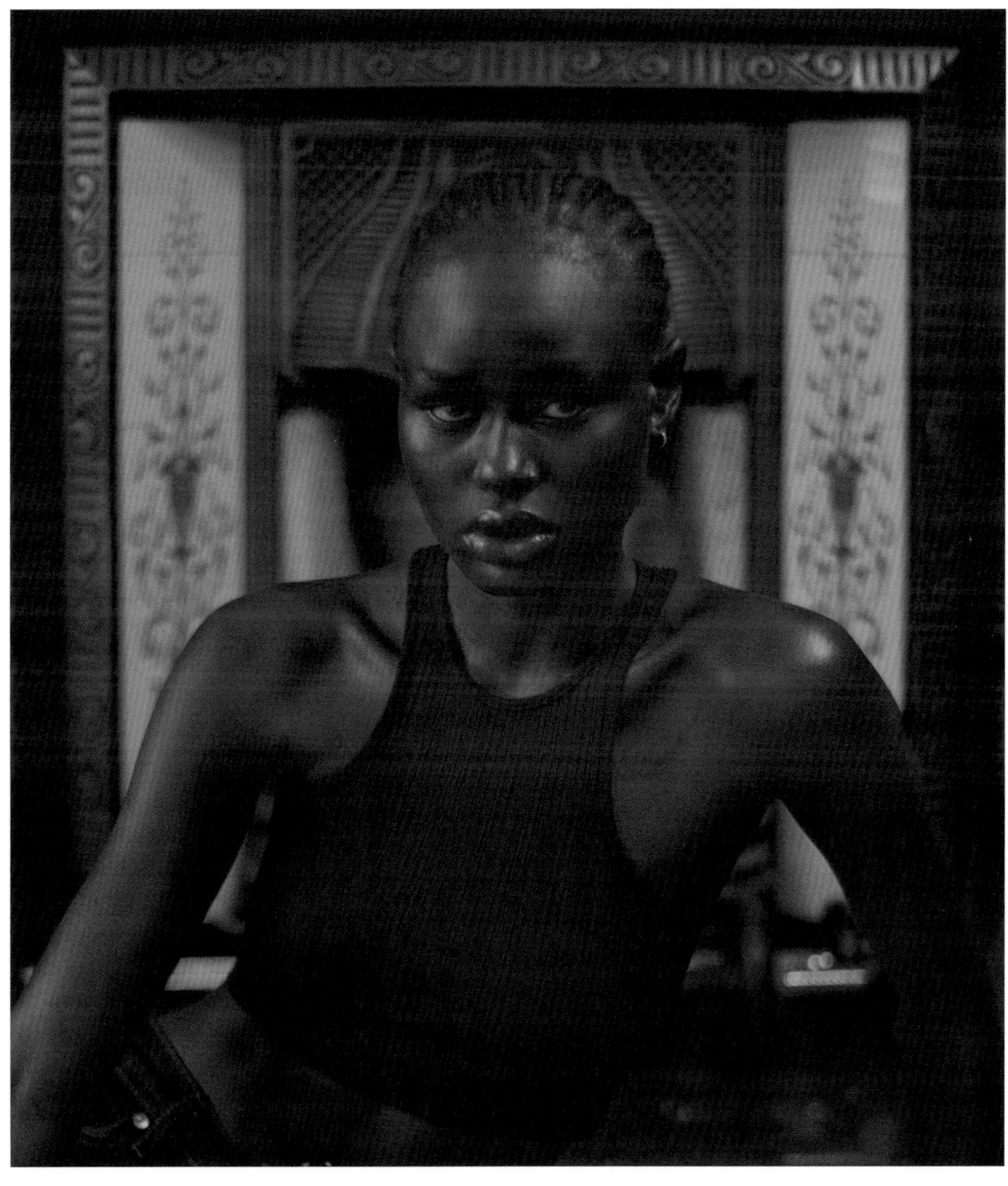

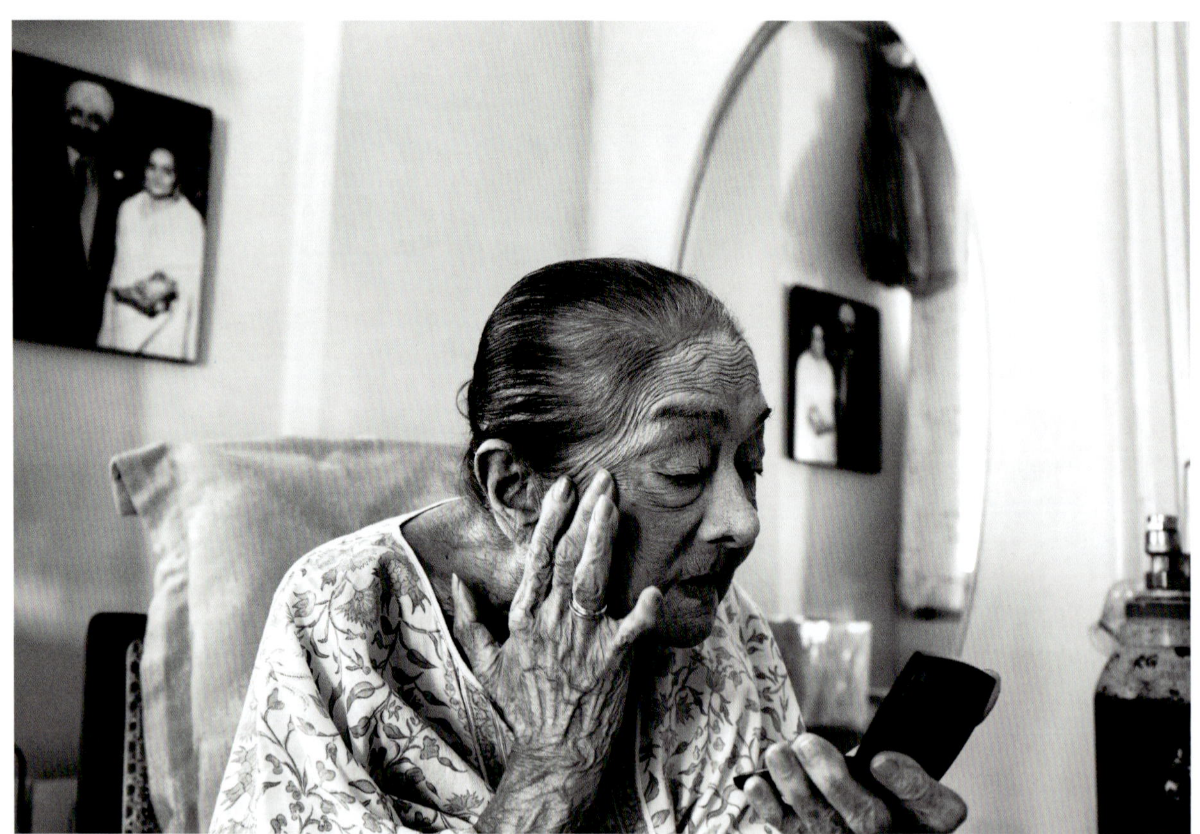

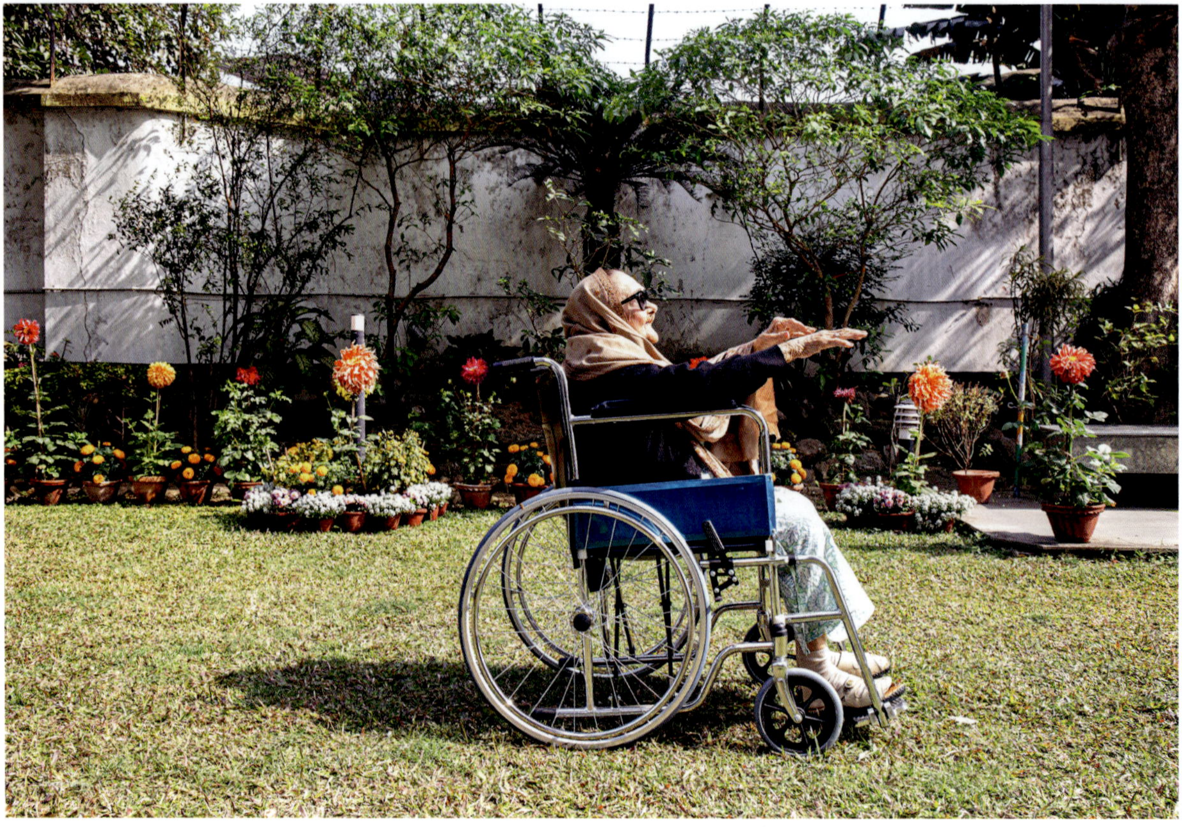

Jasmeen Patheja

Inderjit Kaur, 2023
Indri and the Winter Sun, 2023
From the series *Indri*
Inkjet prints

Jasmeen Patheja has been photographing Indri, her much loved grandmother, for over 20 years. In one image, she captures her going outside to 'greet the New Year and the winter sun'. Patheja's images admire and celebrate Indri's sense of routine, ritual and daily practice, while providing positively affirming portraits of old age. Patheja founded Blank Noise, a community project that confronts street harassment in India. The significance of her engagement with others is visible in this joyful collaboration with her grandmother.

Sophie Ebrard
Issam, 2024
From the series *My friend Achraf*
Chromogenic print

Ôussáma, reclining on horseback and lit by vehicle headlights, is a friend of Achraf – a long term collaborator with photographer Sophie Ebrard. The image is from the series *My friend Achraf*; it explores young adulthood among a group of male friends on the West Coast of Morocco and has followed their transition through their childhood and teenage years. Urban signifiers appear out of place in this portrait; while the young man's casual manner indicates his ease on horseback, his beauty and elegance enhanced by the shimmering equine rump.

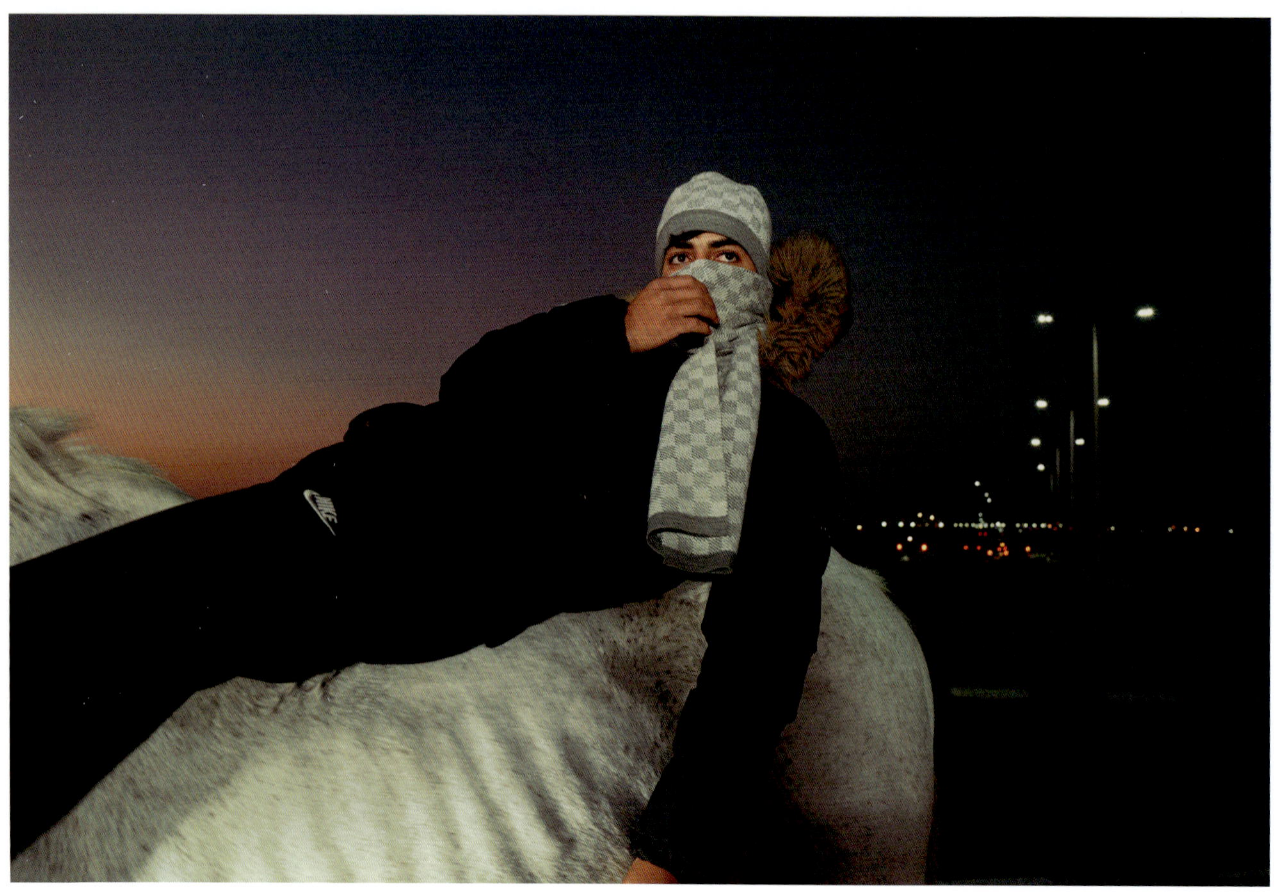

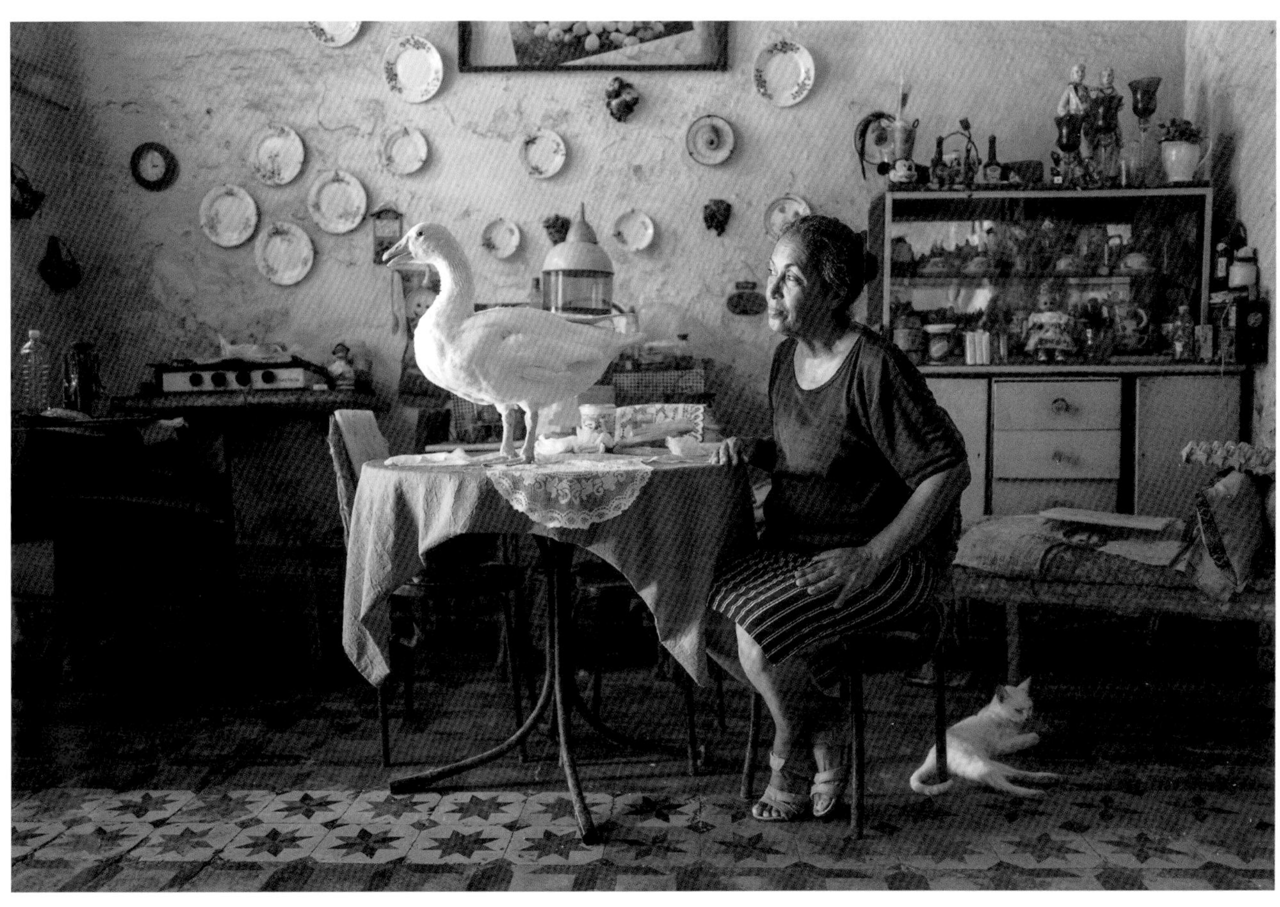

James Clifford Kent

Cary, Axiuli & Haytoo at home in San Leopoldo,
Havana, Cuba, 2023
From the series *¡No hay más na'! (there's nothing left)*
Inkjet print

This photograph comes from a series which explores
Cuban communities facing socio-economic crises.
James Clifford Kent captures 65-year-old Cary living
alone with her animals in a home in Havana, Cuba,
which once functioned as her family's laundry business.
Cary's children are among the many who have emigrated
in search of greater economic conditions. The sense
of seeking out a brighter future is echoed in Cary's look
beyond her pet goose and into the light.

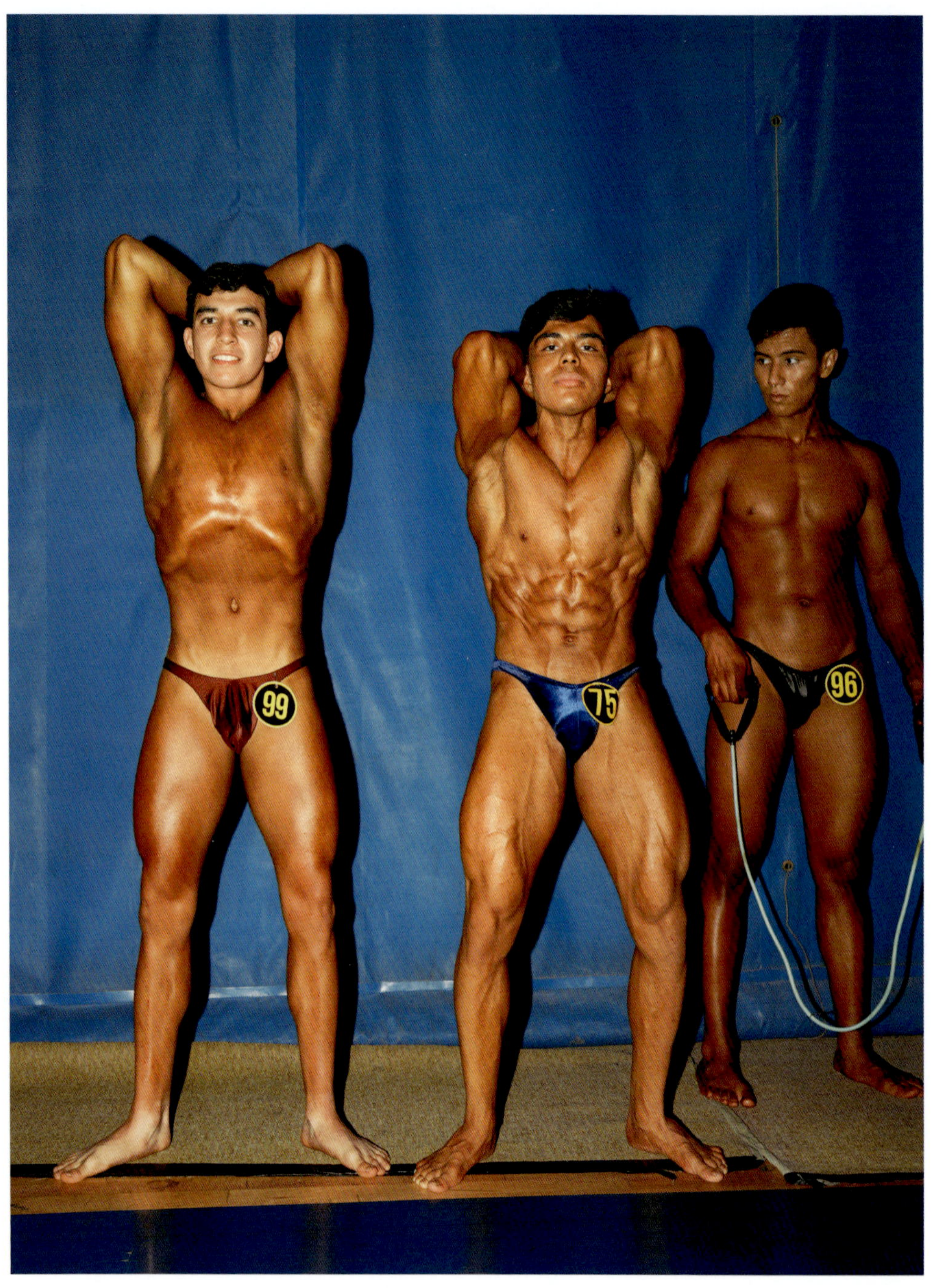

Francisco Rosas Rangel
Bodybuilders Backstage, 2024
From the series *Baja Bodybuilders*
Inkjet print

Two young bodybuilders snap into position for the camera, while preparing backstage for the Mr Baja Juvenile Bodybuilding Competition in Mexico. Francisco Rosas Rangel finds fascinating the display of masculinity and performance that bodybuilding offers; it visually makes for a series of curious details, such as the stark white feet and face, and the subtleties in posing. Meanwhile, the third contestant concentrates on final reps for crucial last minute muscle definition before going onstage.

Anoush Abrar
Untitled, 2023
From the series *Hereo*
Inkjet print

Invited by a member of the community, Anoush Abrar was given rare access to a group of women who had been attending a Herero funeral in the Kunene region of Namibia, Southern Africa. Originating from an ongoing documentary project, exploring influences of modernity within the community, the assured stance of the women in their finery defies a nostalgic view. They are empowered women who combine traditional Herero clothing – their hats as a nod to their respect for cattle – with statement heels and bold framed glasses. The three modest tents provide a muted backdrop to the colourful sitters. Abrar was a prizewinner in the 2013 and 2018 Photo Portrait Prize.

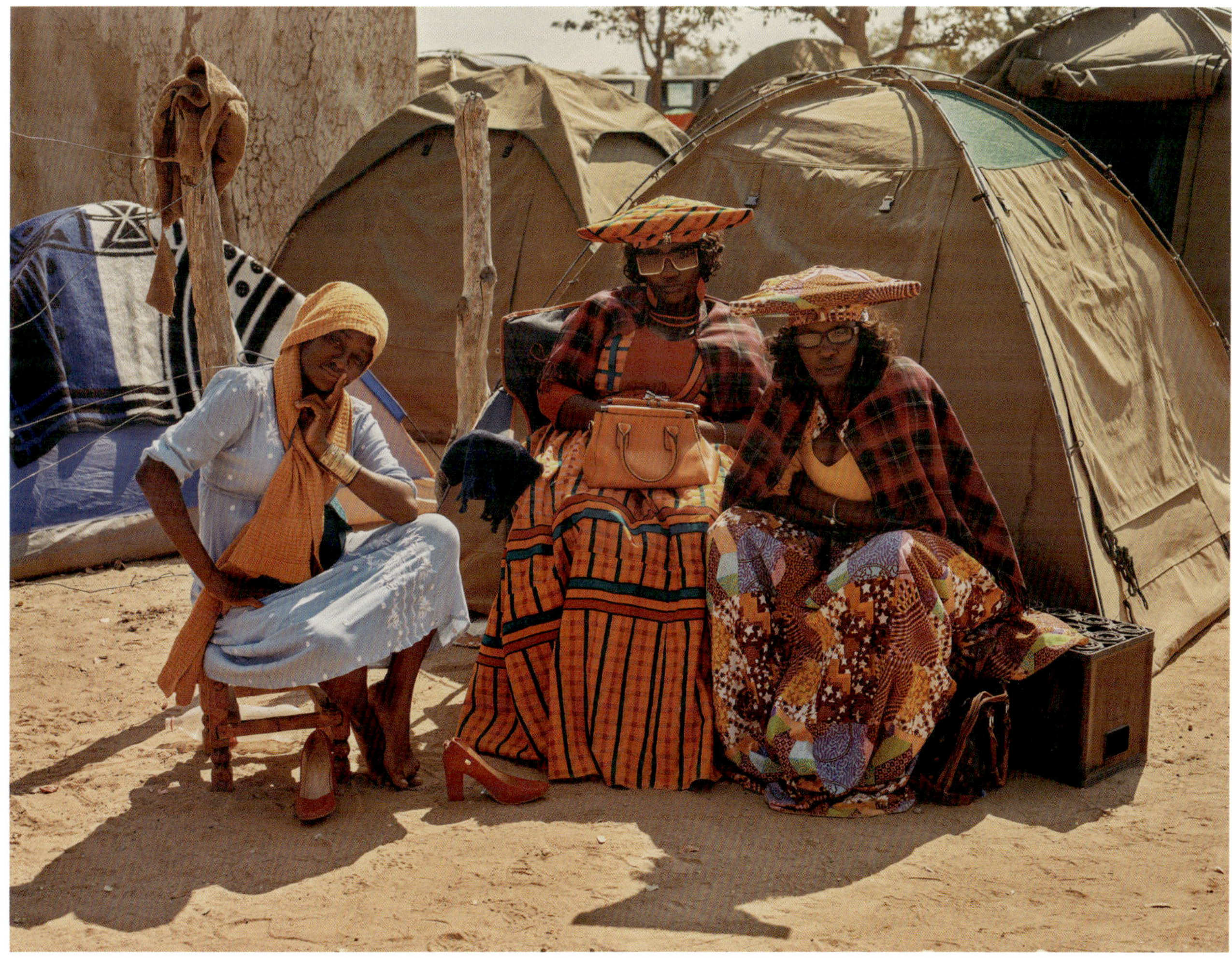

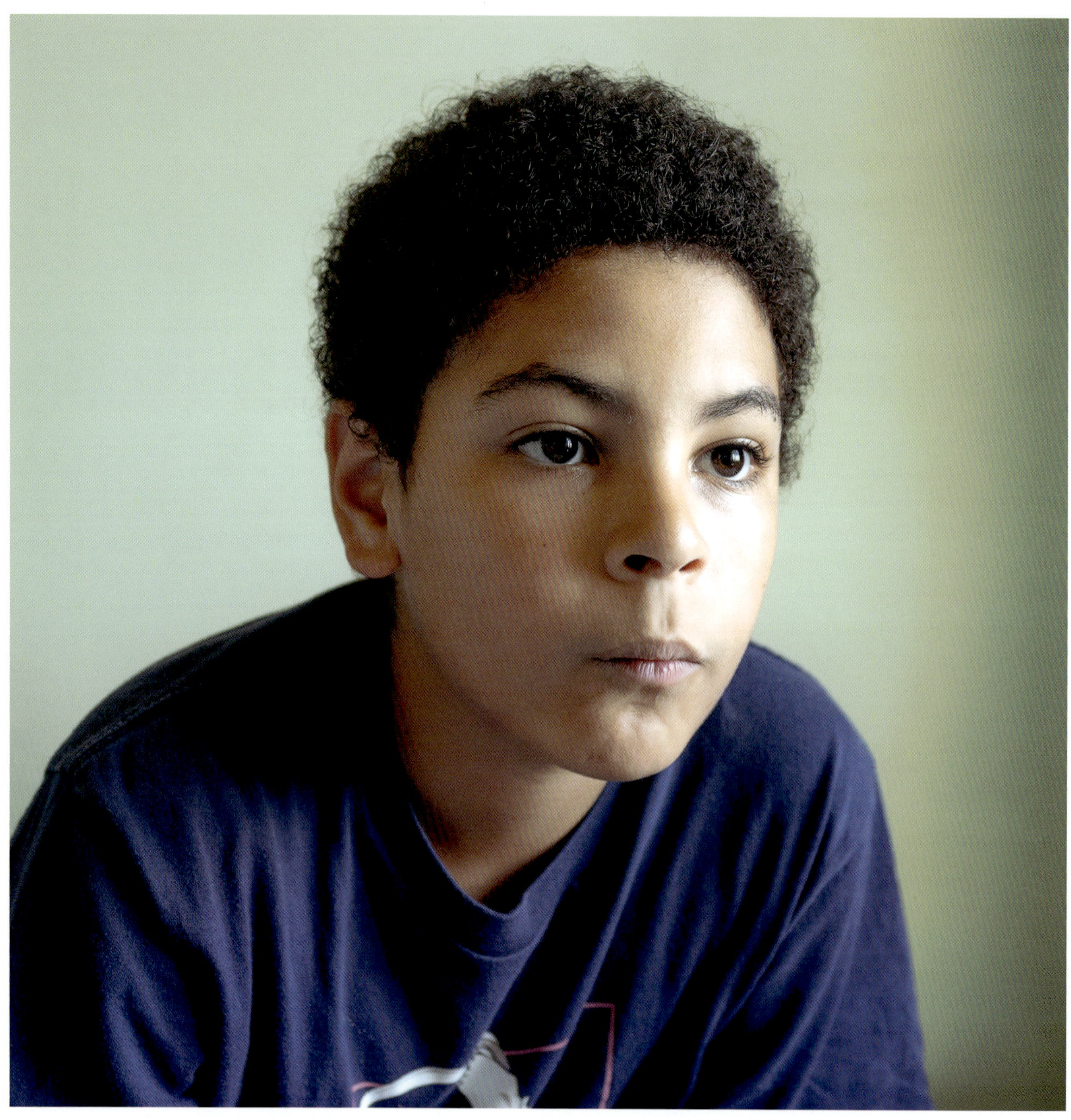

Kate Brownbill
Game Face, 2023
Inkjet print

Kate Brownbill captures a quiet portrait of her son, focusing on his wide eyed, sharp concentration as he leans into his video game world. The lack of decoration or detail, with the pale background, suggests that everything he needs can be found in the digital space in front of him. The image acts as an entrance into the world of fantasy and is a reminder of the power of play and escape. As the photographer explains, 'In these moments, his face is completely unselfconscious and unique to that moment - his *Game Face*.'

Phil Sharp

Grace Cooper Milton, 2024
Inkjet print

This portrait was made as 'Lilac Wine' by Nina Simone
was playing and Cooper Milton, an actor and friend of Phil
Sharp, was moved to tears. Sharp uses music frequently
in his sittings, which he celebrates as imprinting a moment
between two people. Nuanced, ever-changing natural
light is Sharp's preference, and he allows time for evolving
interactions with the sitter, avoiding excessive direction.
His influences range from cinema to Dutch master paintings.

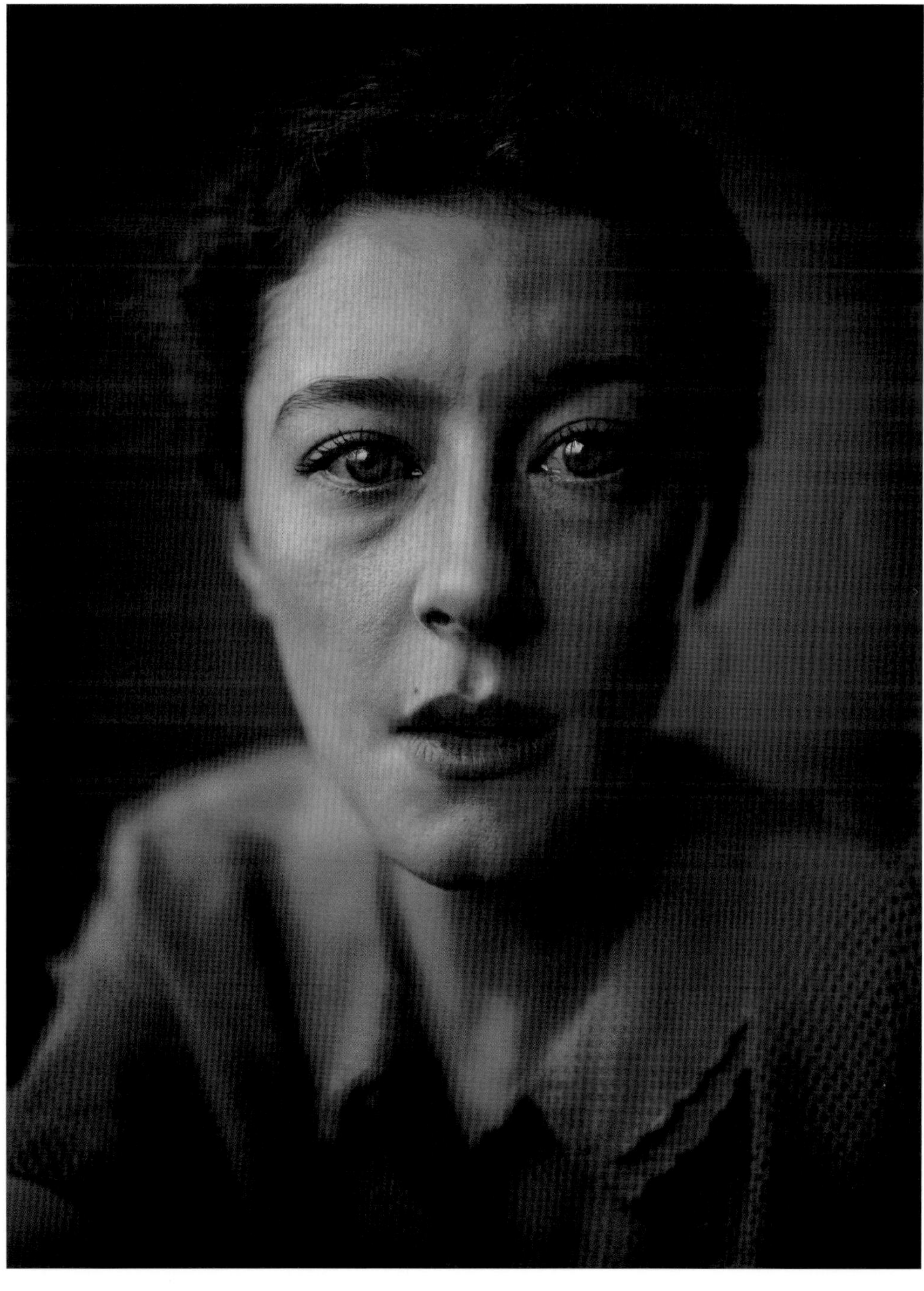

Jacek Davis

Chlo Mydia, 2023
From the series *Whiplash*
Inkjet print

Jacek Davis invited Chlo to create a series of images to explore the feelings of a person behind a drag performance. In wearing only undergarments and a wig, a sense of vulnerability is created. Davis captures the drag performer to engage with the difficulty in balancing self-expression and societal pressures, where feelings bounce between 'a powerful force' and 'identity confusion.' The visual jarring of part human, part disguise, alongside the rigid pose, creates an unsettling image that draws attention to this struggle.

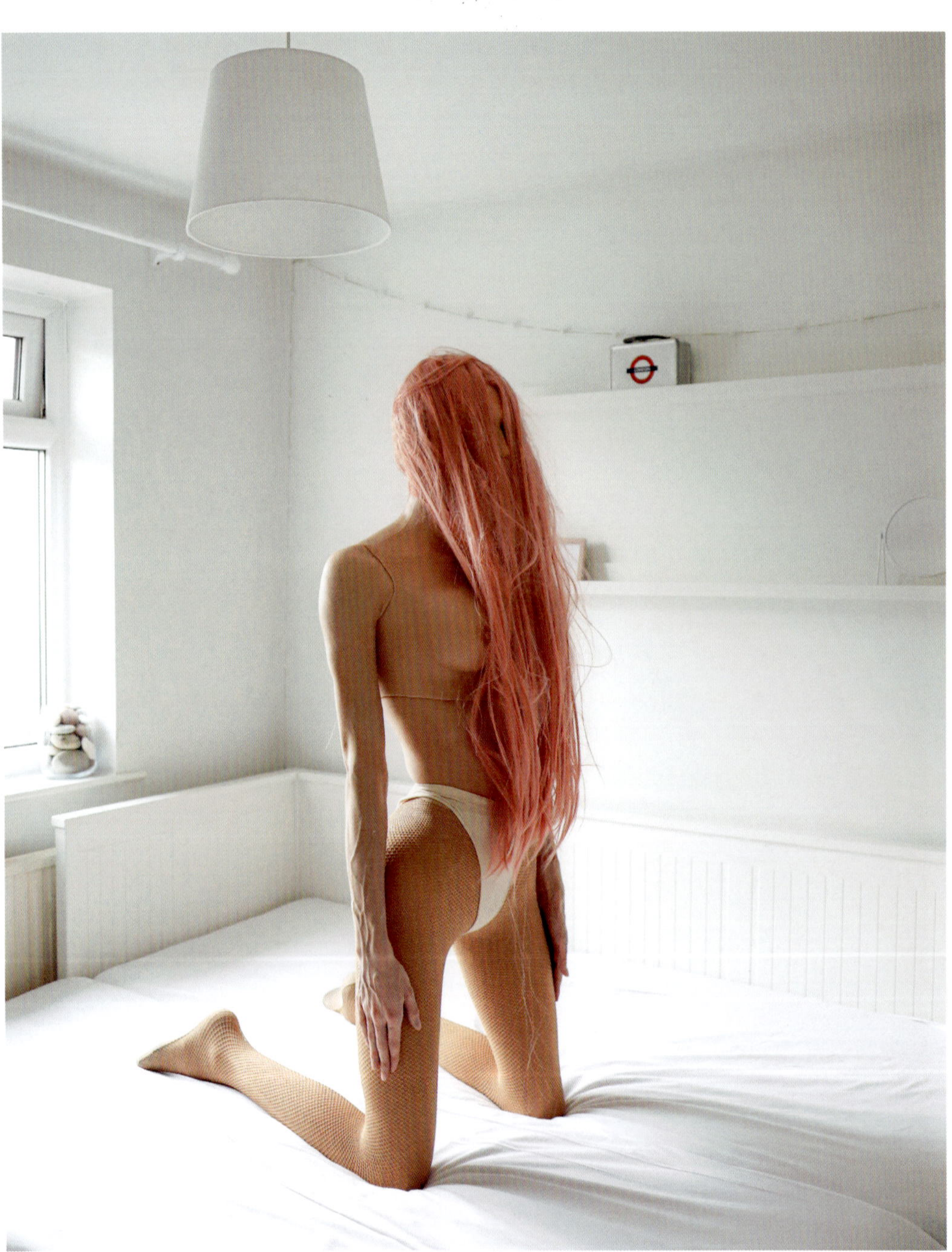

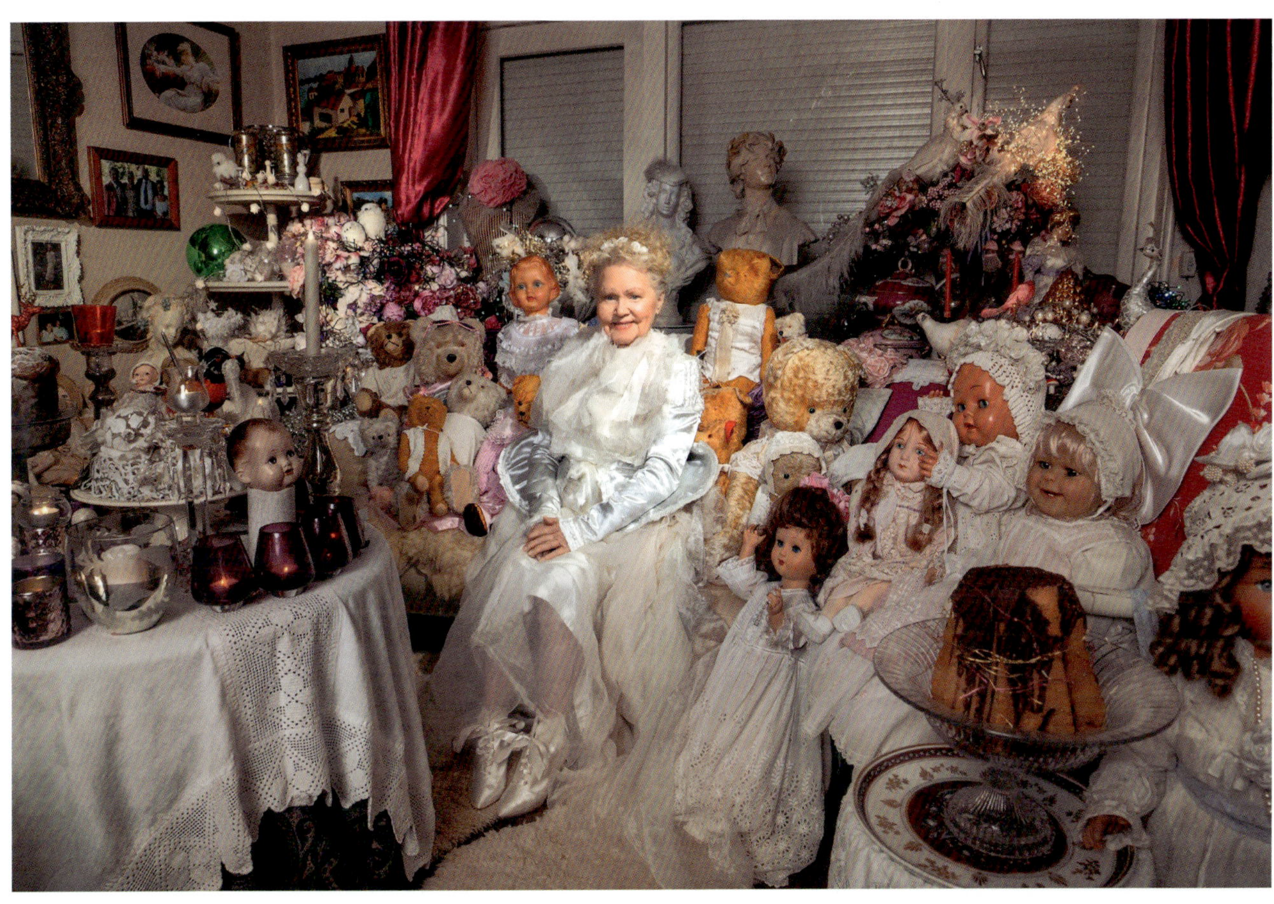

Harmen Meinsma

Roosje, 2024
Inkjet print

Curiosity piqued by a local newspaper article, Dutch photographer Harmen Meinsma visited 90-year-old Roosje, a well known figure of optimism in her hometown of Middelburg, the Netherlands. Roosje enjoys dressing for each day in a 'party' dress from her collection. An active collector of vintage dolls and antiques, she is depicted as a vital part of this visual spectacle. Working with hair and makeup artist Ed Tijsen, stylist Showroom41 and in post-production with Jan Daniel Wolters, this shoot encompasses a collaboration that resulted from a feeling of 'mutual connection' between sitter and photographer.

Nick van Tiem

Slo, Mzwandile and Andile opening the trunk of the
BMW, Kloof Nek Road, 2024
Andile enjoying the last rays of sun in the Broke Boys
kitchen, Woodstock, 2024
From the series *It was never meant to be easy (2024)*
– A Broke Boys story
Inkjet prints

Nick van Tiem's portraits speak of his long term collaboration with the Broke Boys collective: where five friends from Cape Town, South Africa, countered financial insecurity with brotherhood, aspiration and creativity. In van Tiem's portrait of Andile, his face masked by a deep shadow, the fashion branding 'BROKE' is just visible – an ironic symbol of the collective's self-made success. In another image, they are seen from the boot of Andile's car that they drove between cities to sell their new branded clothing. The dramatic graphic diagonal framing alludes to this momentous experience.

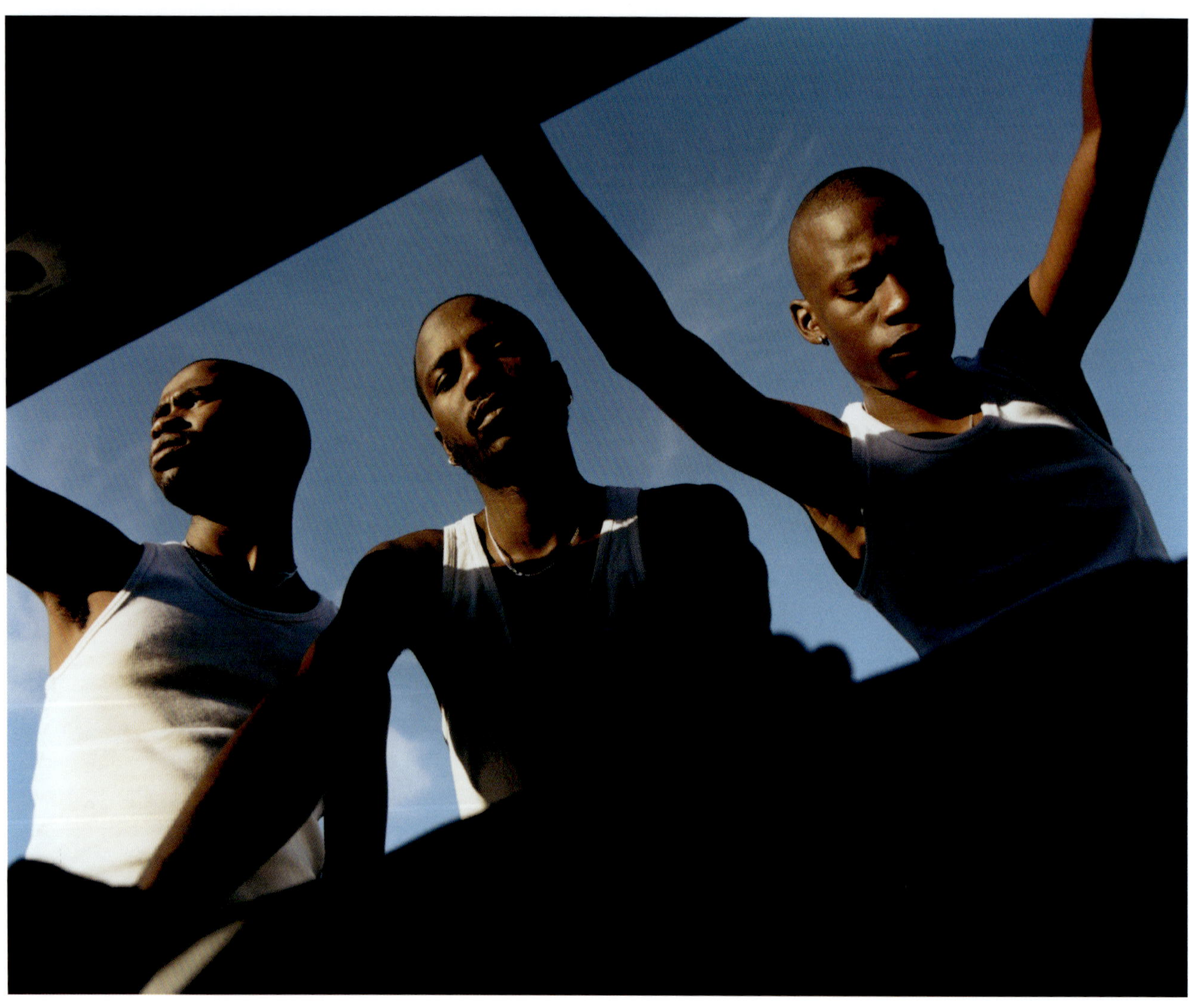

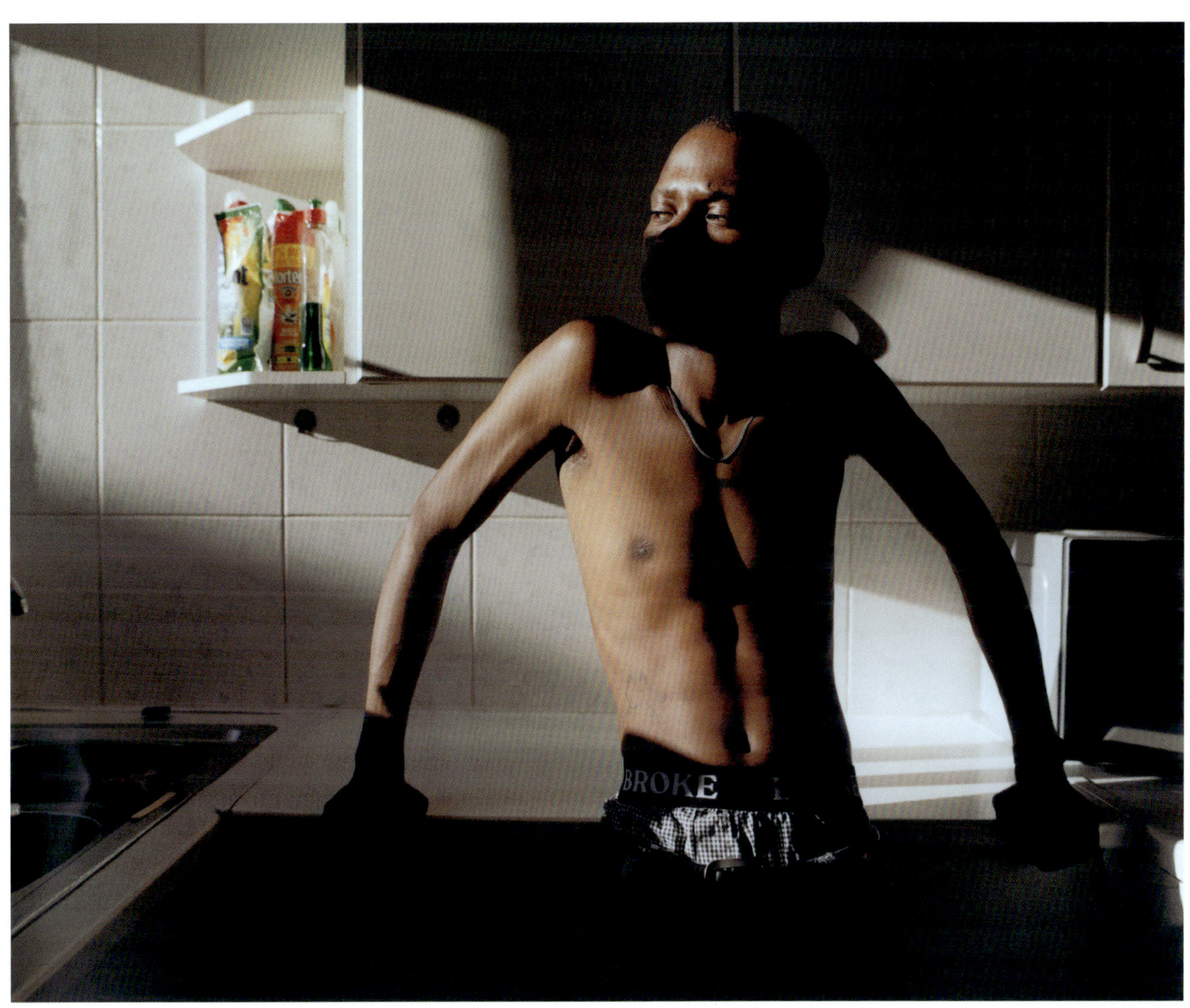
BROKE

Yan Wang Preston

Yan Wang Preston
After 'Olympia, 1863', 2023, A Self-Portrait, 2023
Gelatin silver print

A famous painting by Édouard Manet is paired back to its basic elements: the model's reclining pose and confrontational gaze. This photograph was created as a test shot for the series *After 'Olympia, 1863'*, in which Yan Wang Preston restages the painting from a feminist and decolonial standpoint. Here, the absence of a backdrop reveals the photographer's studio, transforming the test shot into an insightful self-portrait. 'I realised that this image is the truest representation of myself as a female and non-white working photographer.'

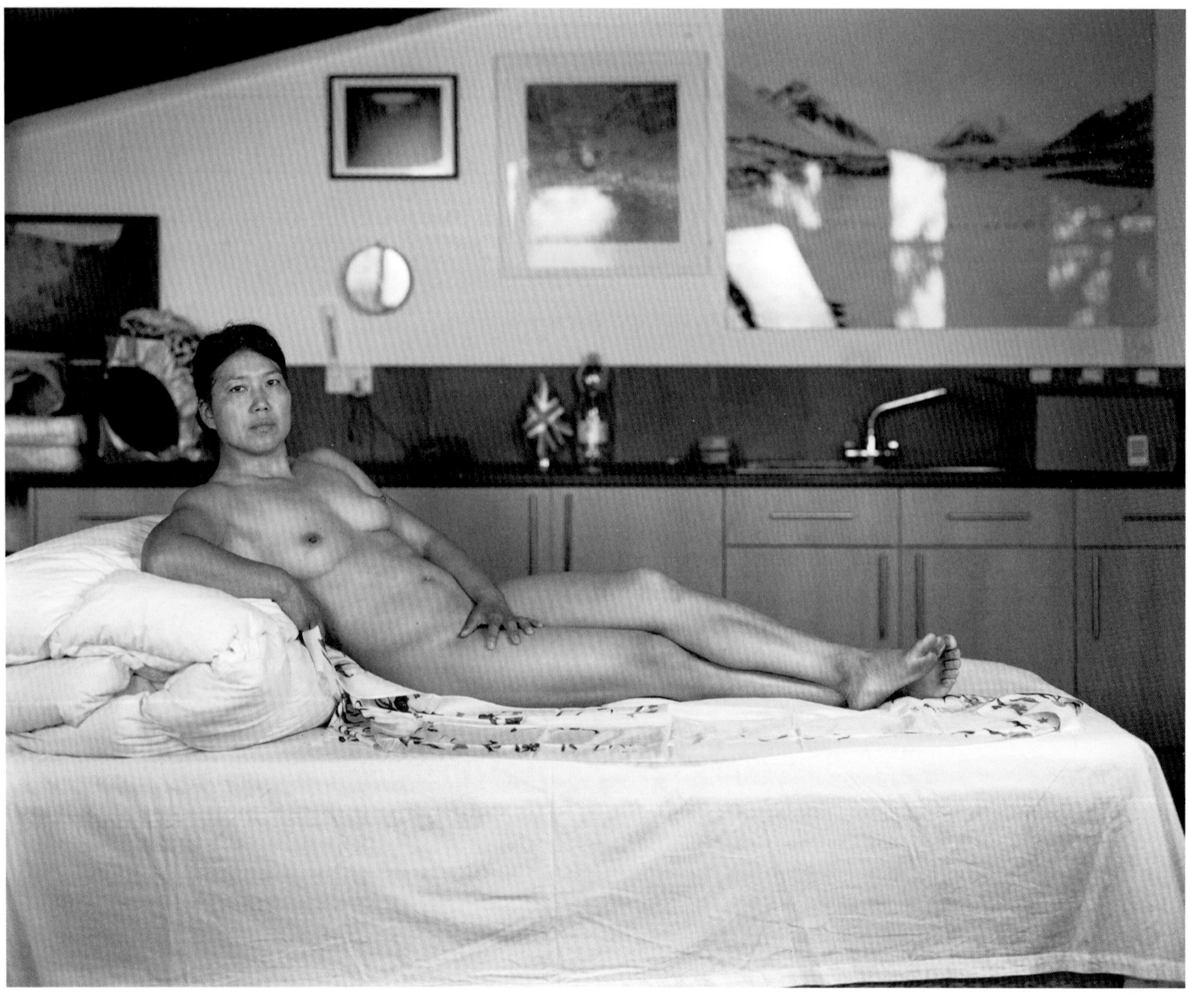

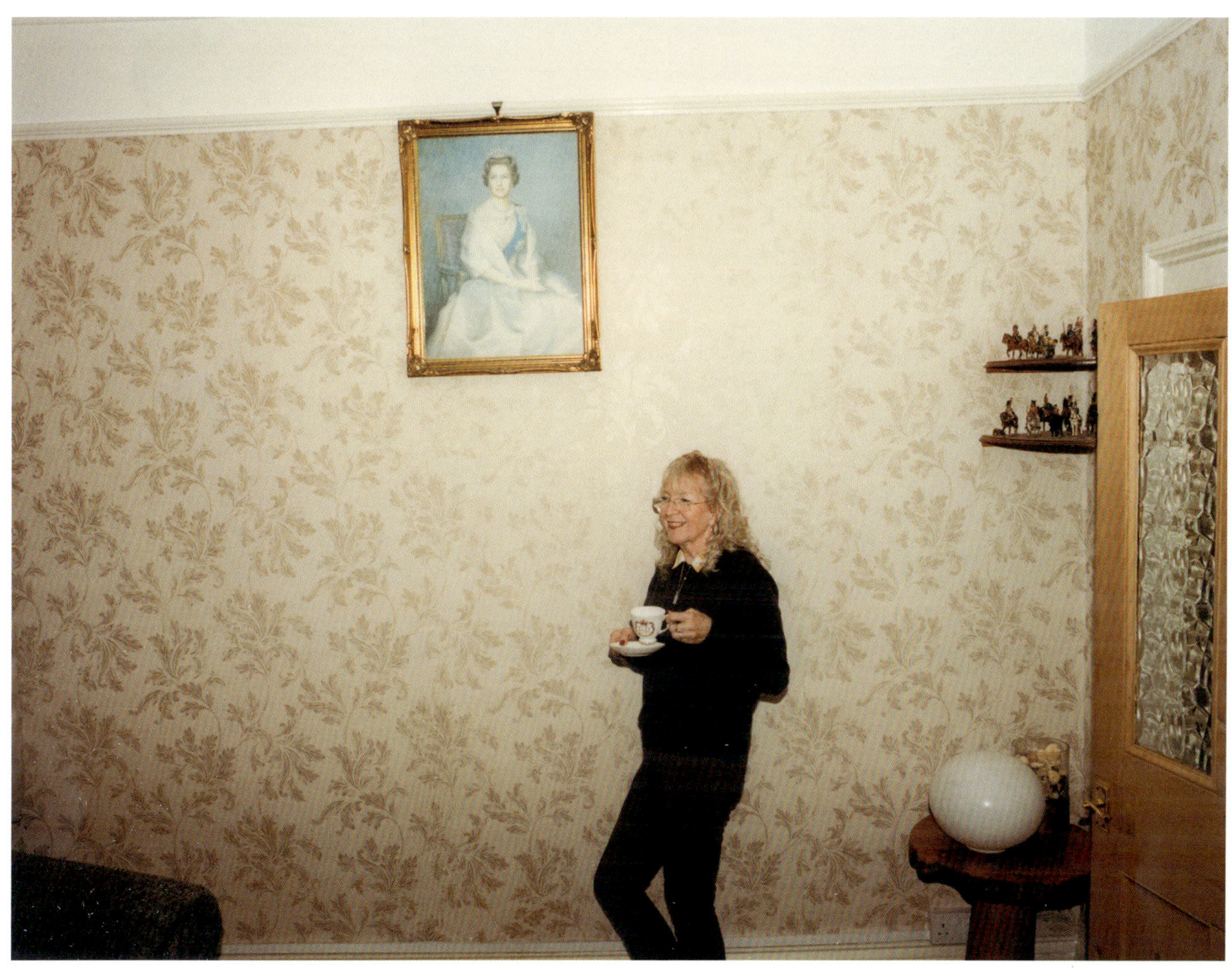

Roo Lewis
Christine, Sewing Machinist, 2023
Chromogenic print

Christine, a former sewing machinist for fashion brand Belstaff, is depicted in the living room of the house that was the former Belstaff premises. She is framed by a teetering faded portrait of Queen Elizabeth II and a troop of soldier figurines. Roo Lewis was commissioned by the fashion brand on its centenary to photograph legends, ambassadors and historic workers to celebrate their roots in the North of England. Over a cup of tea, Christine spoke fondly of working alongside her sisters before the Longton factory closed in the 1990s. Today, she said 'when I go anywhere, I go up to people: "I like your jacket, I like that shirt". They look at you funny I say: "It's all right – I used to work 'em"'.

Wayne Hanson
Tobias, coming back from church, 2024
From the series *Locals*
Inkjet print

Driving through Willesden, London, Wayne Hanson noticed a shop closed for redecoration, its windows awash with old newspaper print. Struck by its potential as a photographic backdrop, he returned that Sunday morning with his old Hasselblad camera in hand. Within moments, Tobias passed by on his way home from church, his light blue tracksuit perfectly echoing the tones of the newsprint. 'I approached him, and he was very open, exuding a quiet confidence that I believed would translate into a strong portrait'. Photographing within his local community, Hanson asks viewers to appreciate the richness of human experience on our doorstep.

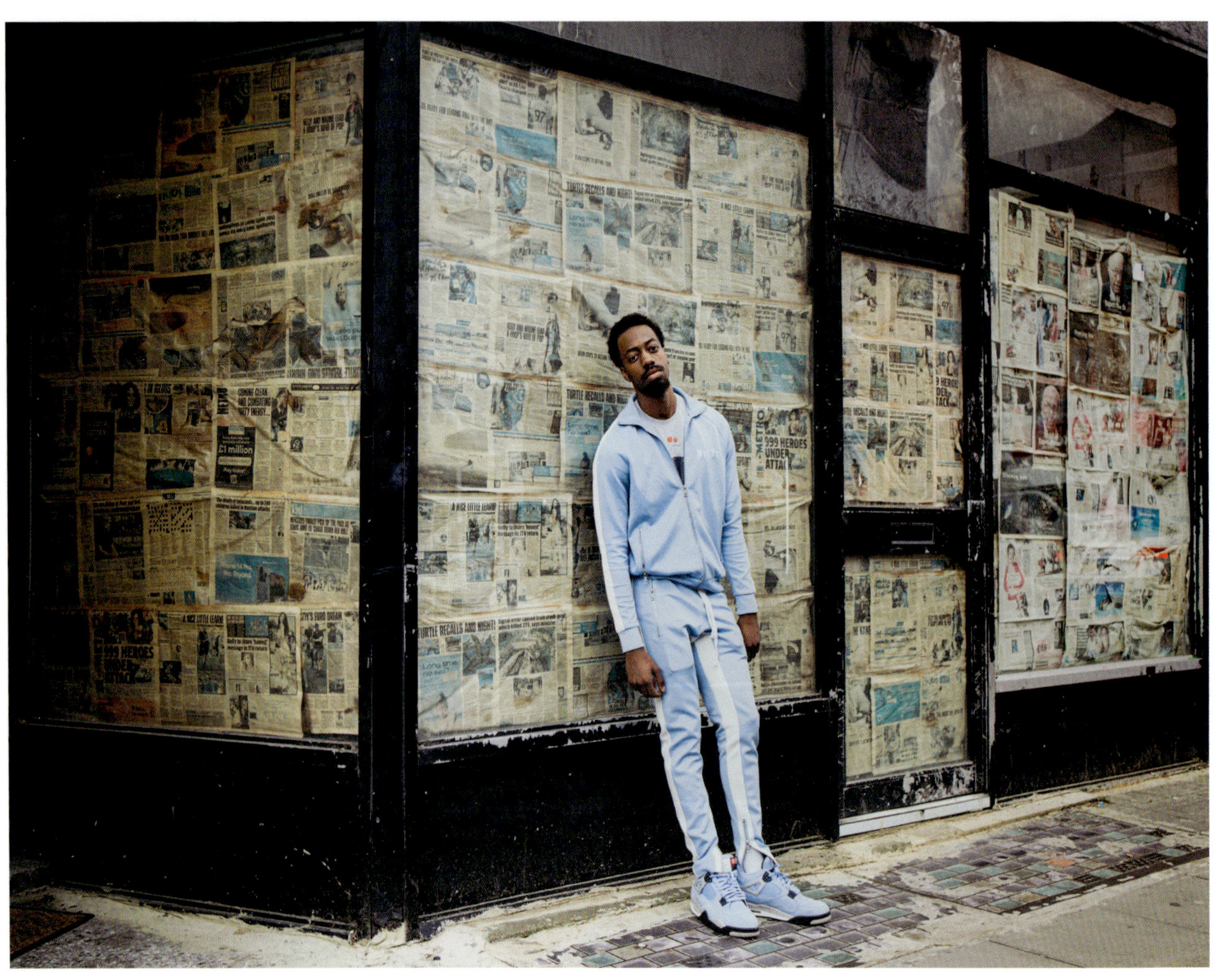

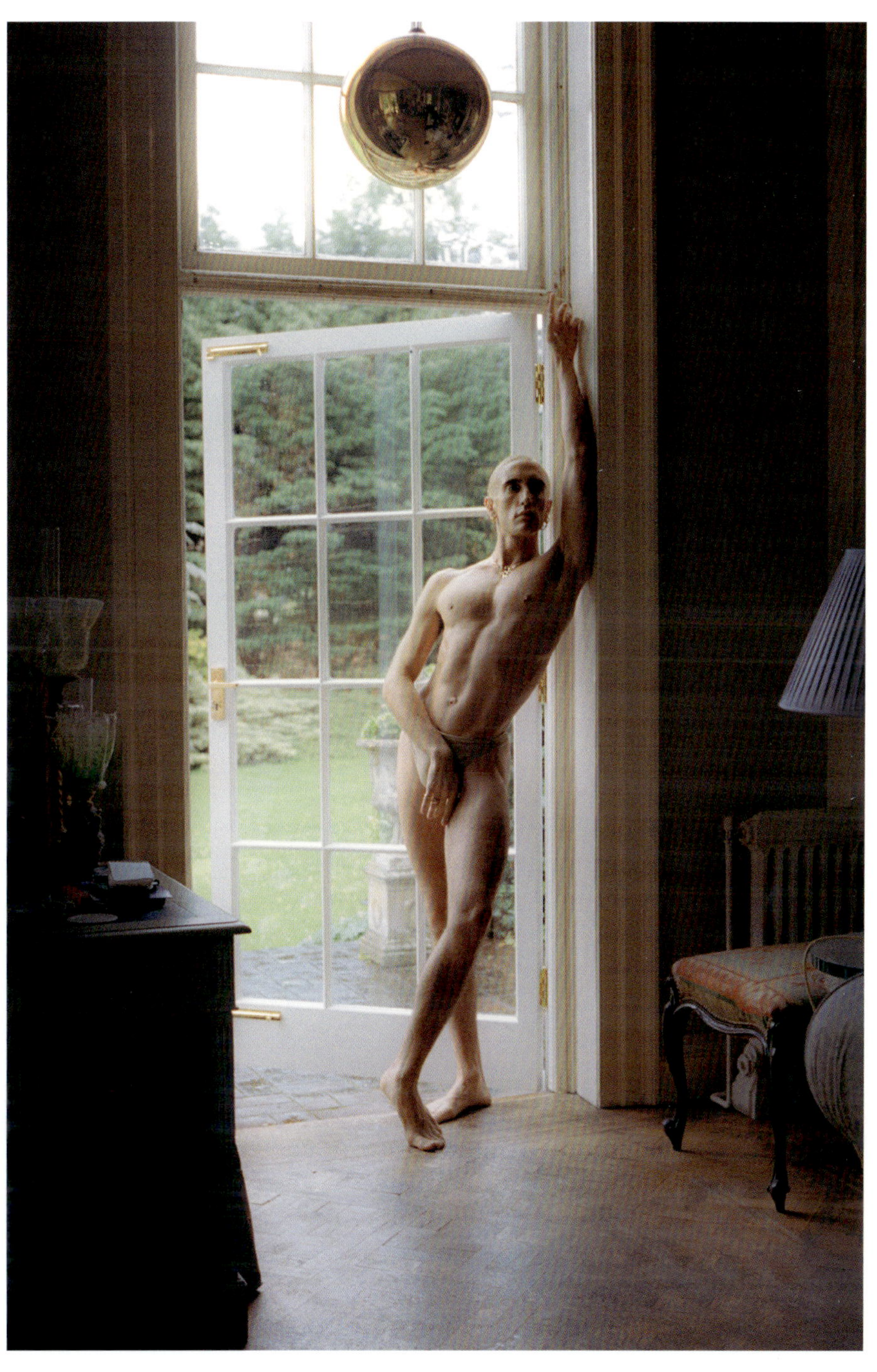

Hidhir Badaruddin
Ed Munro, 2023
Chromogenic print

The touches of gold details in Hidhir Badaruddin's portrait – hoop earrings, a clustered necklace and a spherical lampshade – bring points of light and lavishness to the interior location. Shooting into the light, the garden scene frames Munro as he fills the height of the doorway. The pose points to his profession as a dancer and choreographer while referencing the architectural eye of the photographer and the interior space.

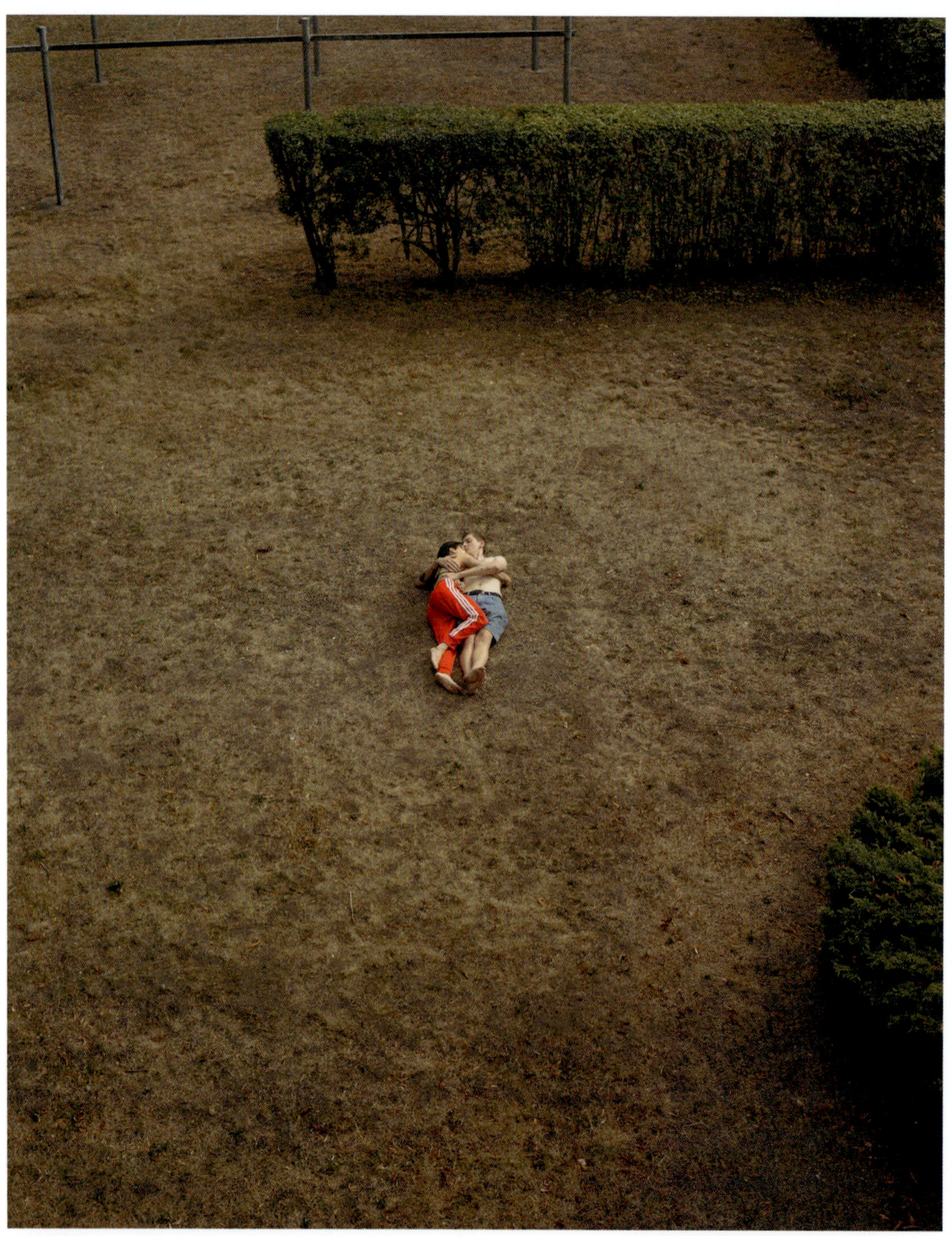

Kovi Konowiecki
Lovers, Leipzig, 2023
From the series *Jüngen*
Inkjet print

At the age of 13, Kovi Konowiecki moved from his home in California to join the TSV 1860 Munich, a professional youth football academy in Germany. *Jüngen* (boys) is an autobiographical coming of age series, following his return to Germany to retrace and capture the tensions of adolescence. A prizewinner of the Photo Portrait Prize in 2016, it was by chance that Konowiecki noticed the tender moment between young, reunited lovers Claudia and Sergej from his balcony. As the sun went down, he captured the embracing couple surrounded by scrubby ground – the hedgerows unifying the almost abstract composition.

Kat Green

Tam, 2024
Chromogenic print

The feeling of being at peace, of being at home, can be felt within the frame of this portrait. Tam reclines amongst trees and greenery, three months after their top surgery. The square of land holds potential in the form of their future home which will be built here. While the sky is slightly overcast and it is not possible to see what has caught Tam's attention in the distance, Kat Green successfully manages to capture a moment of change, hope, reflection, and momentum.

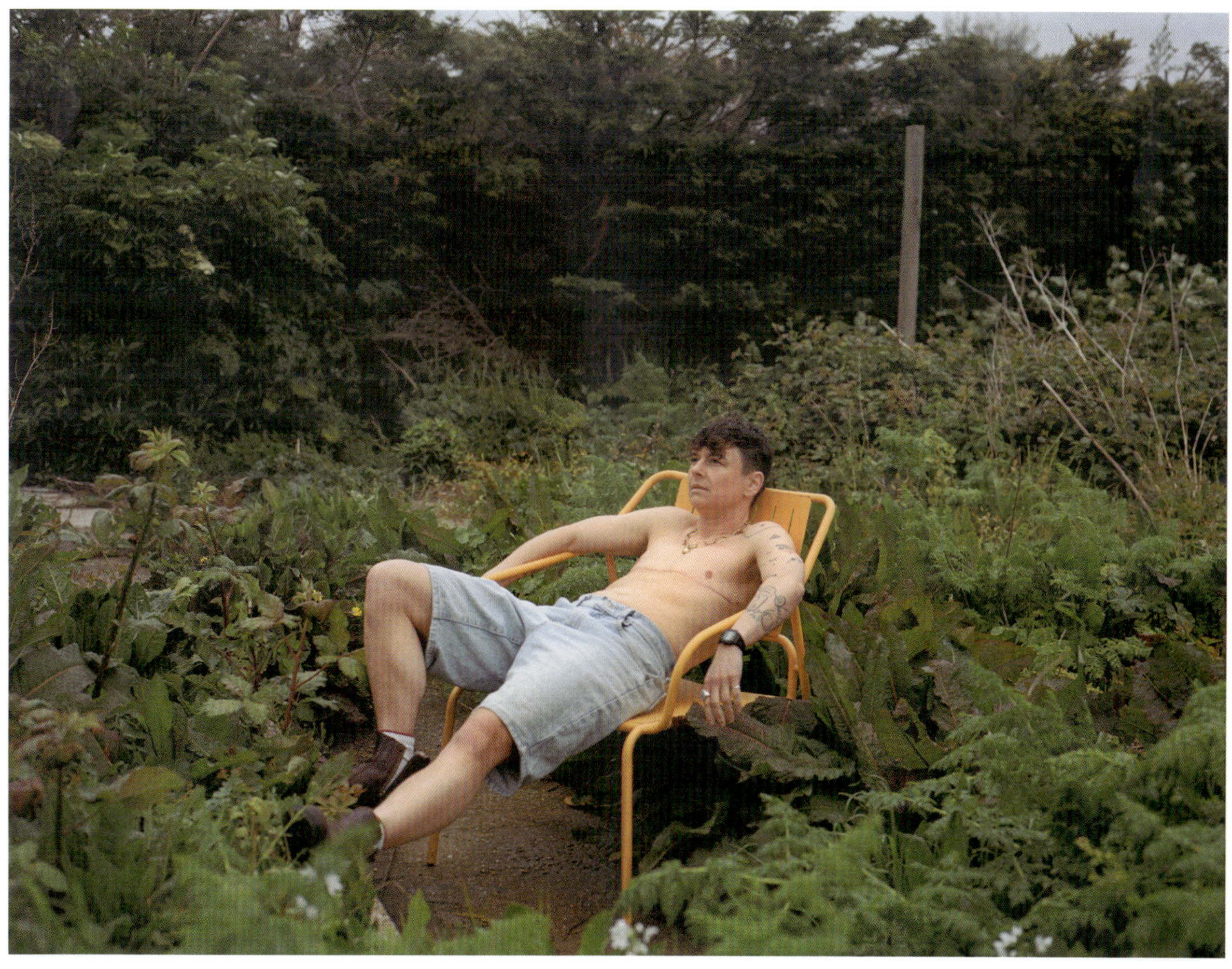

Christian Sinibaldi

Phuong from the Saigon Beast, 2023
From the series *Passion for Cheers*
Inkjet print

In this richly layered portrait, the main narrative focuses on the young sitter, a member of the Vietnamese Saigon Beast cheerleading team, while the background details fill in the space. A rooster is held in its cage by the weight of a food container, while similar cages are piled up to house a small array of plants, with other slices of life jostling behind. Phuong holds space in the middle of this scene, alert and ready to compete. This is one of many images from a series in which Christian Sinibaldi travelled to several countries to 'document the skills, ability, sweat and passions' of those involved.

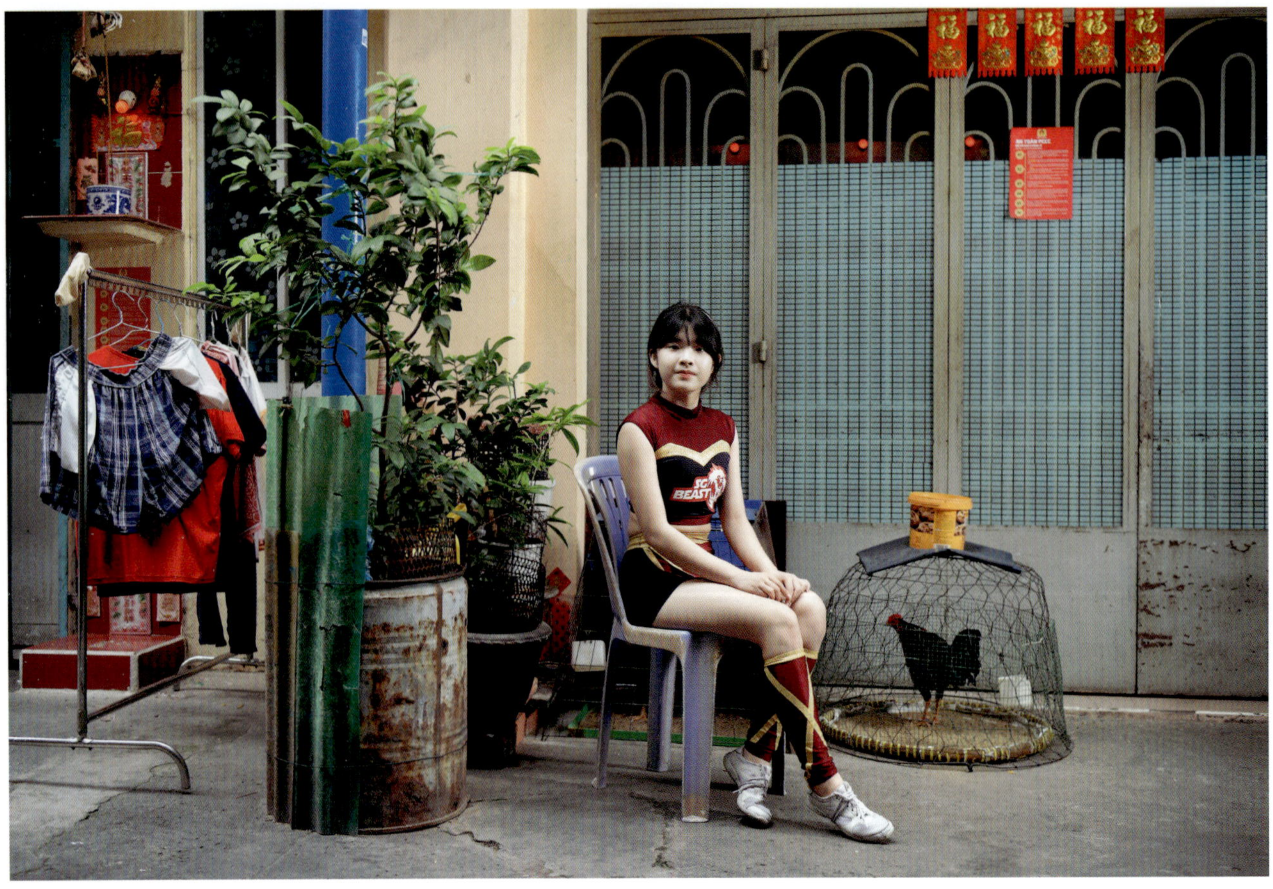

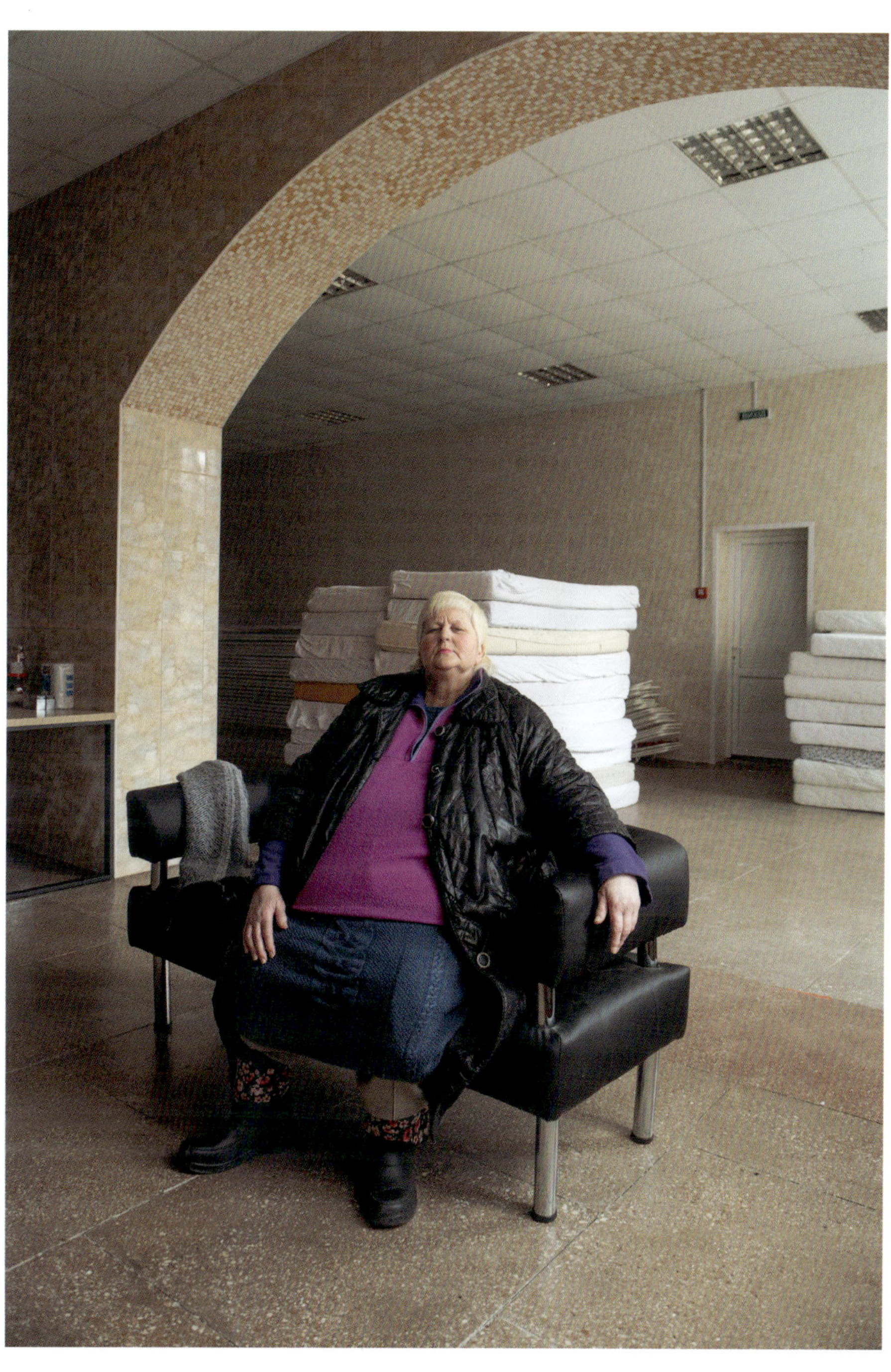

Hannah Maule-ffinch

Tamara at Poltava, Ukraine, 2023
Inkjet print

Tamara raises her chin to meet our gaze. Seated firmly on the black sofa, she appears assured, yet the towering pile of mattresses behind her hint at precarious circumstances. Hannah Maule-ffinch met Tamara whilst on assignment in Ukraine, photographing the crowded women's centre where Tamara had been living for eight months since fleeing the bombing of her hometown. In this desperately bleak setting, her purple jumper and bright pink lips read as a small act of defiance.

Tanmay Saxena
Ardhnarishwar, 2023
From the series *Postcard Inlandia*
Chromogenic print

Tanmay Saxena photographs his friend Gaurav in 'a beautifully personal moment'. Born in India, Saxena has lived in London for the last 15 years, this duality informing his image making. Saxena has titled this androgynous portrayal, made in Muzaffarnagar in Northern India, after the Hindu god who is half man and half woman. Through a series which considers India's socio-economic shift from a traditional rural population, he notes the challenging of gender norms by a new generation 'looking for not only answers, but also wondering if they are asking the right questions.'

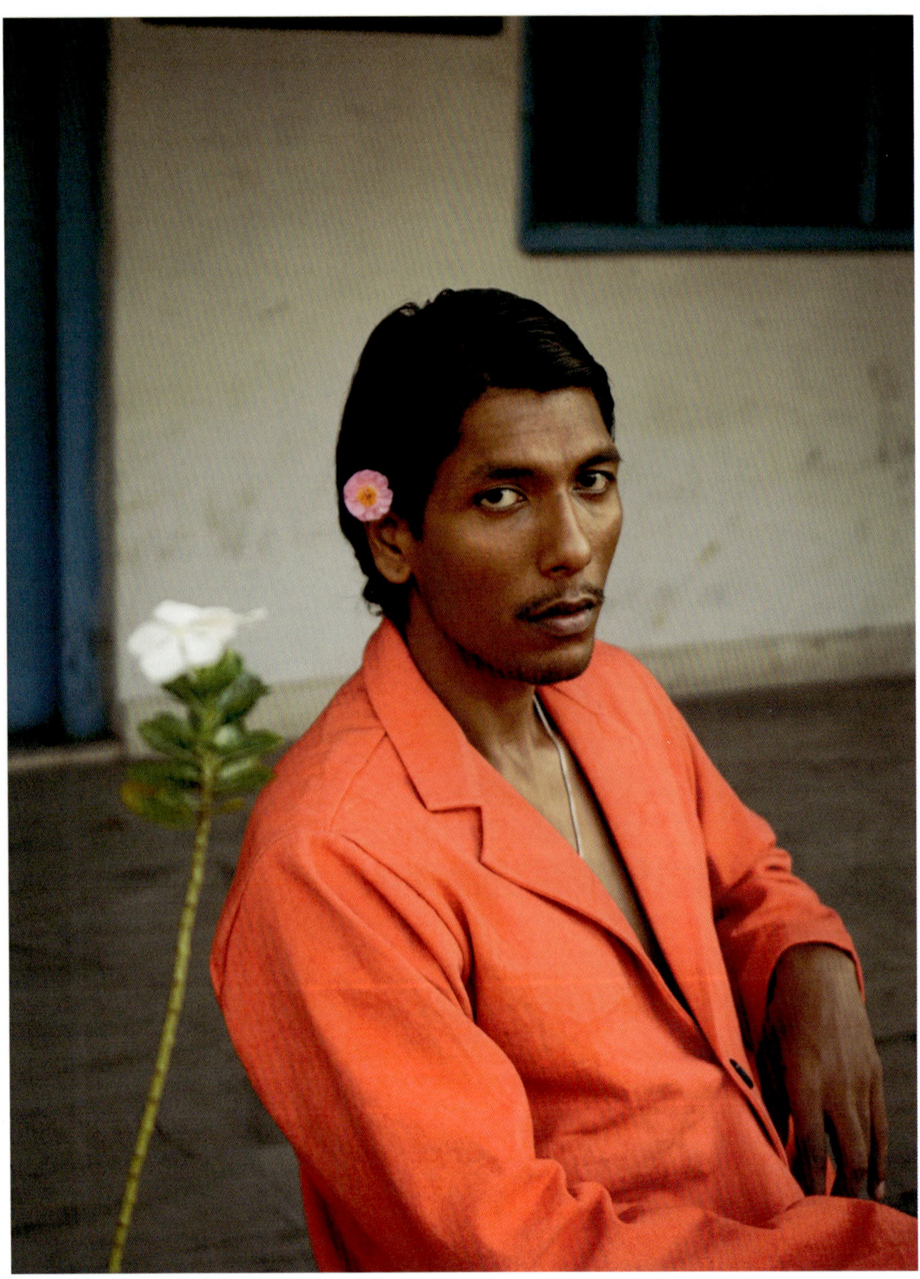

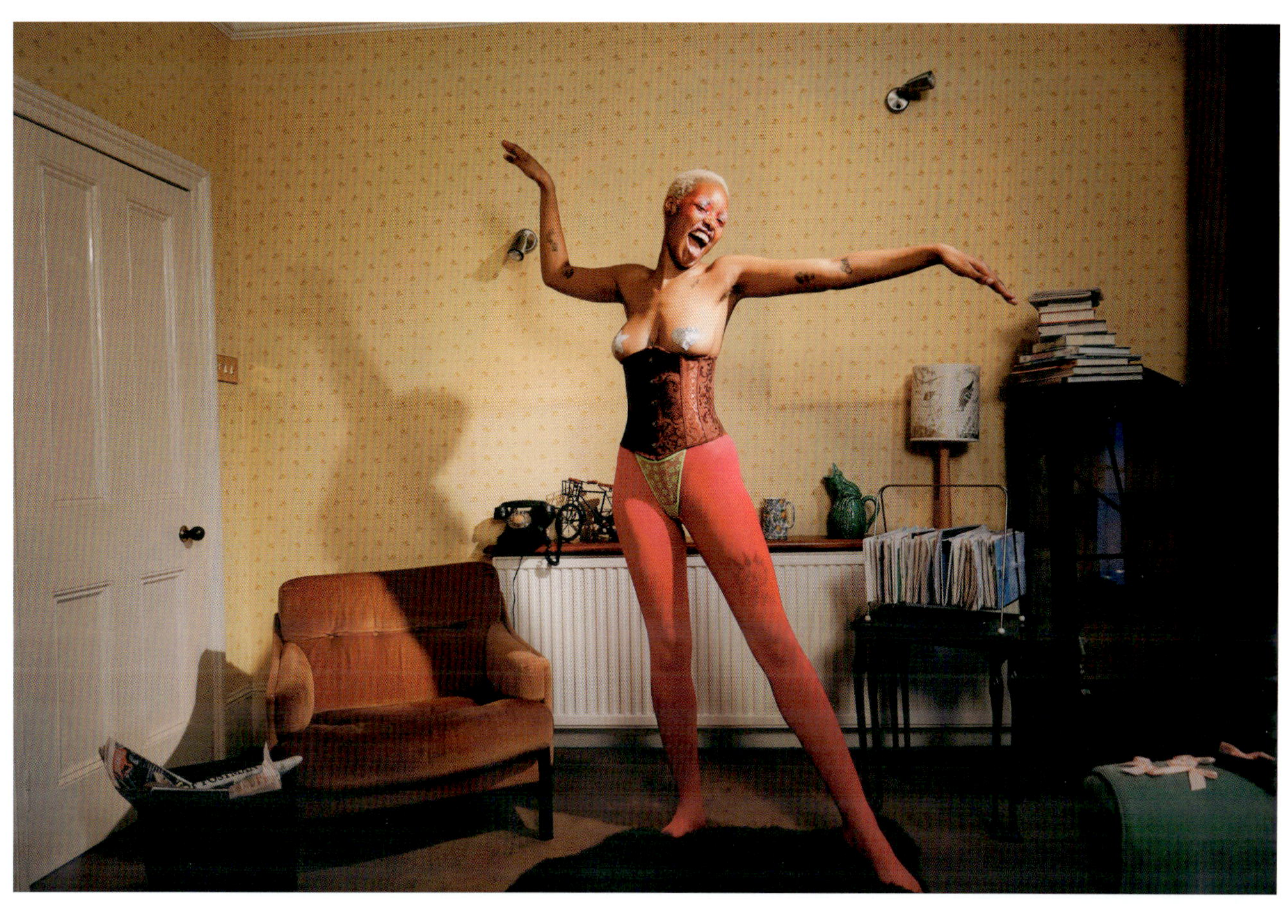

Latoya Okuneye
All eyes on me, 2024
Chromogenic print

This joyous portrait of Zinzi, a model who collaborated with photographer Latoya Okuneye, forms part of a series where the photographer aims to depict the liberation of the body. Central to its narrative is the Black experience and the potential to celebrate the body as universal. Okuneye cast a non-binary model to challenge gender constructs, and this contemporary narrative is juxtaposed by the vintage styled interior. Okuneye notes, '*All eyes on me* aspires to envisage a reality wherein Black people wield unbridled autonomy over their bodies, despite the myriad factors influencing such agency.'

Toks Majek captures 'the style and charisma' of Chicko, a clothes seller in an underground street market in London. Her unique fashion choices and assured gaze combine to give a sense of individuality, captured in this passing moment. Photographed using a 60-year-old lens, Majek prefers to shoot in colour and convert to 'black to white' to create a 'film-like feel' without further editing.

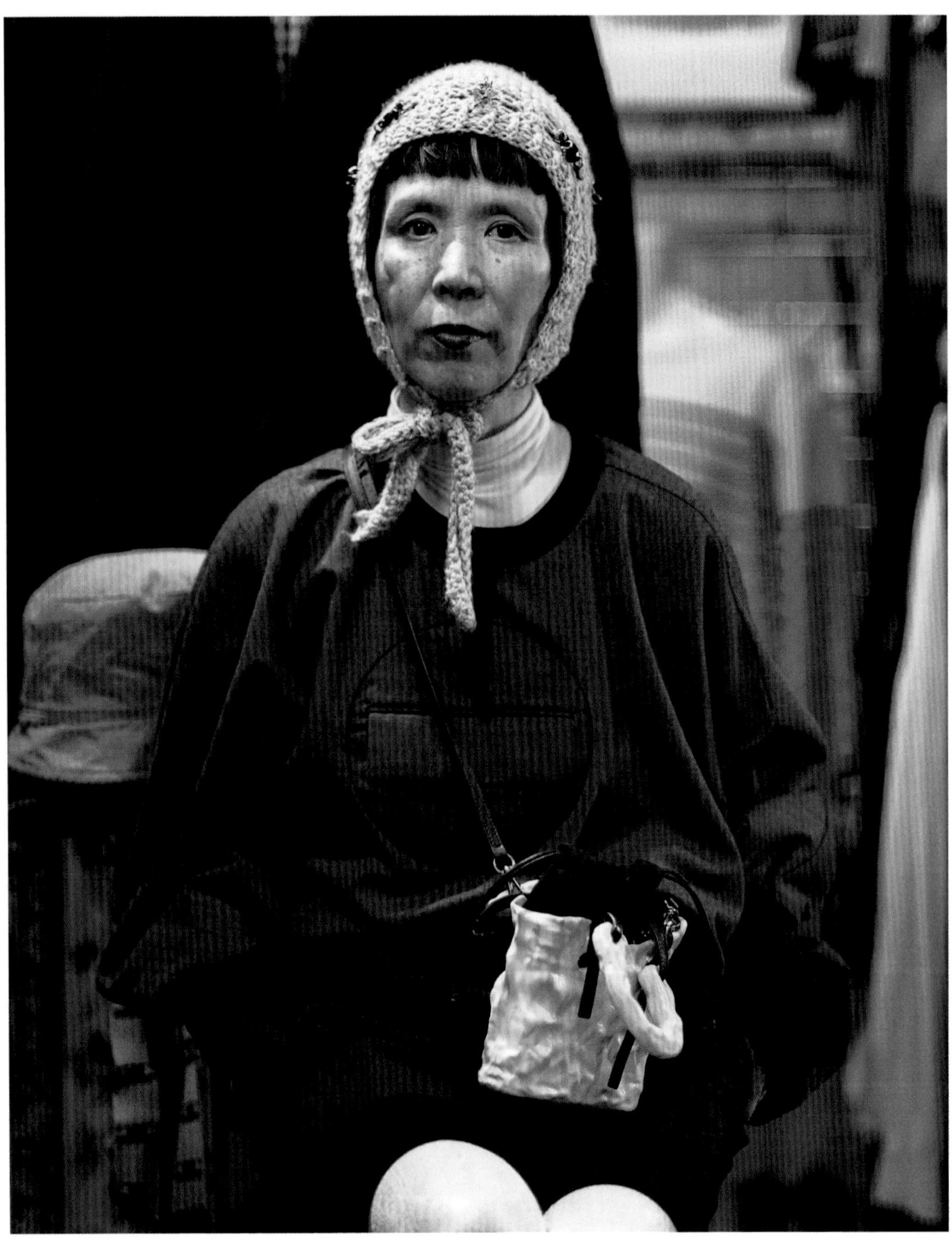

Megan Taylor

Celia and Shay, 2024
Inkjet print

The muted colours and matching blue stripes make for a calming and introspective moment in the lives of these two sitters, with Celia holding Shay in a loose but protective pose. Megan Taylor explains that this is a portrait she had long wanted to create of her sister-in-law, to document mother and son together. Taylor explains that Celia's response to Shay having Down's syndrome was full of love and understanding, with the photograph acting as a testament to that.

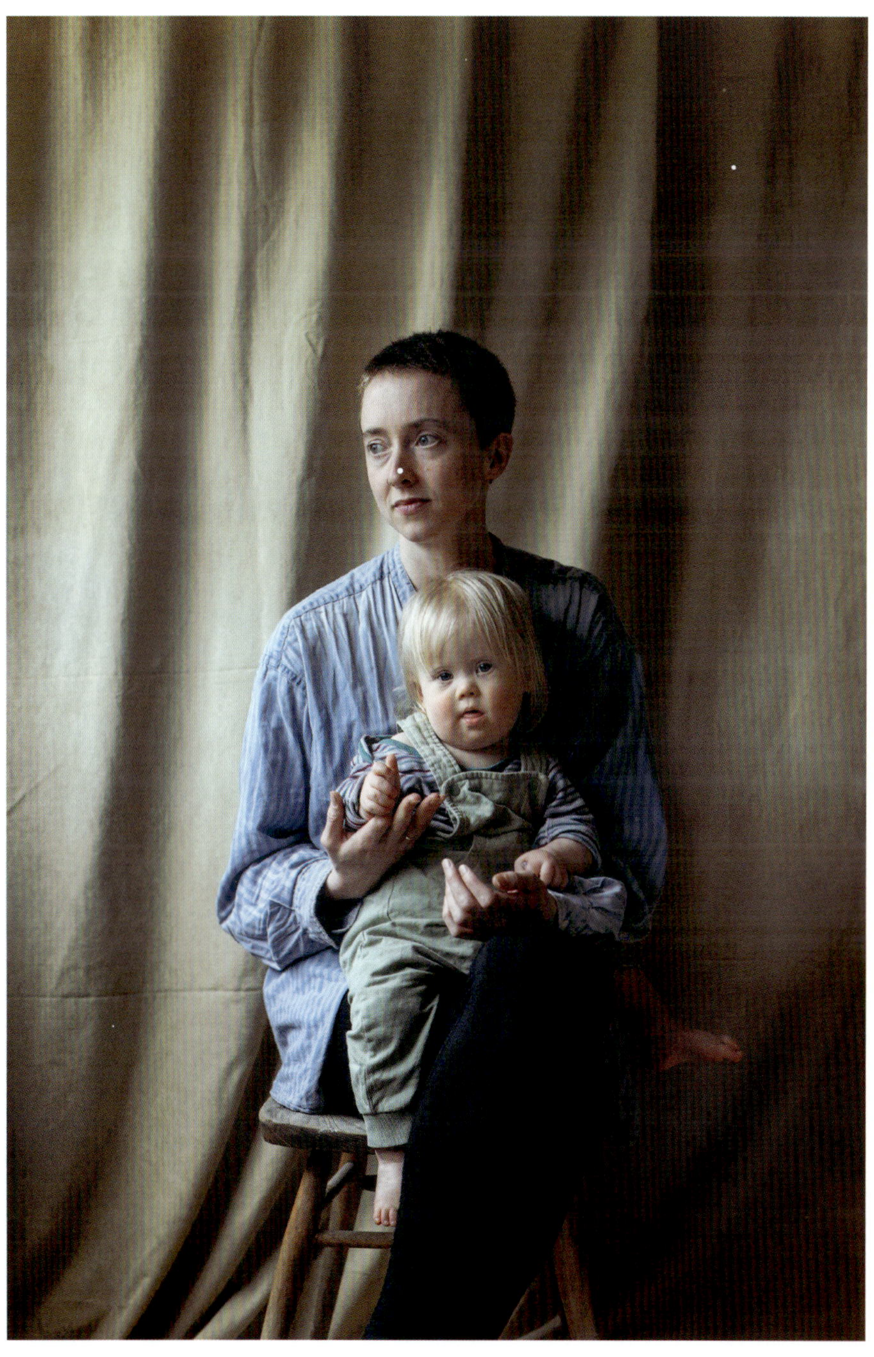

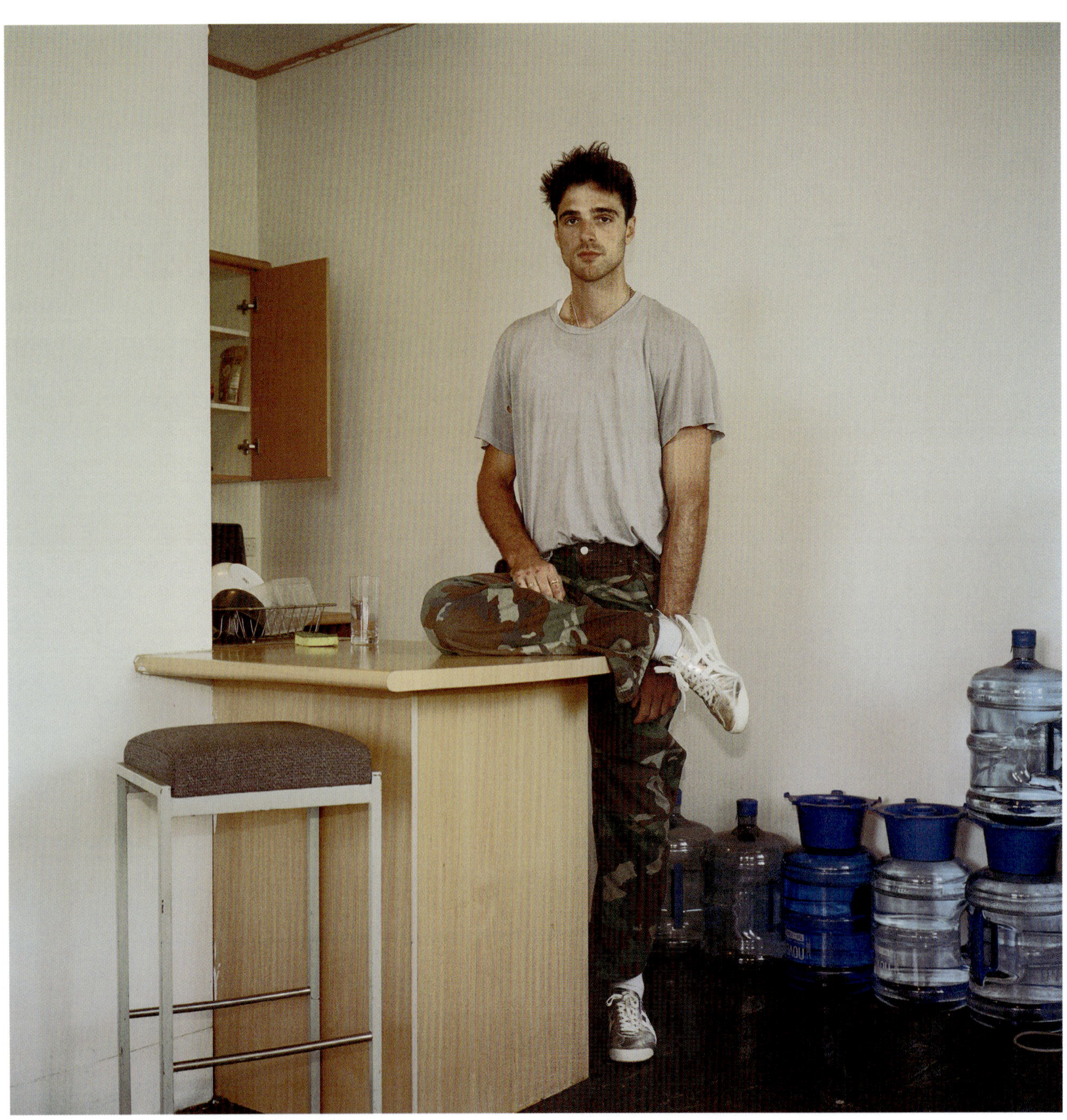

Ingvar Kenne

Jacob Elordi, Actor, Sydney, Australia, 2023
Janelle, Youth Worker, Alice Springs, Australia, 2023
From the series *CITIZEN – portraits since 1994*
Chromogenic prints

Ingvar Kenne's overarching body of work *CITIZEN* spans nearly 30 years and 70 countries. He uses the same camera, lens and film to democratise his sitters. Despite his acting plaudits, Jacob Elordi appears against a modest backdrop; his impressive pliability adding a surreal element to the mundane setting. Kenne's portraits are often reactive, a result of everyday encounters; Janelle was his Airbnb host on a visit to Alice Springs, Australia. Kenne describes his portraits as the result of curiosity.

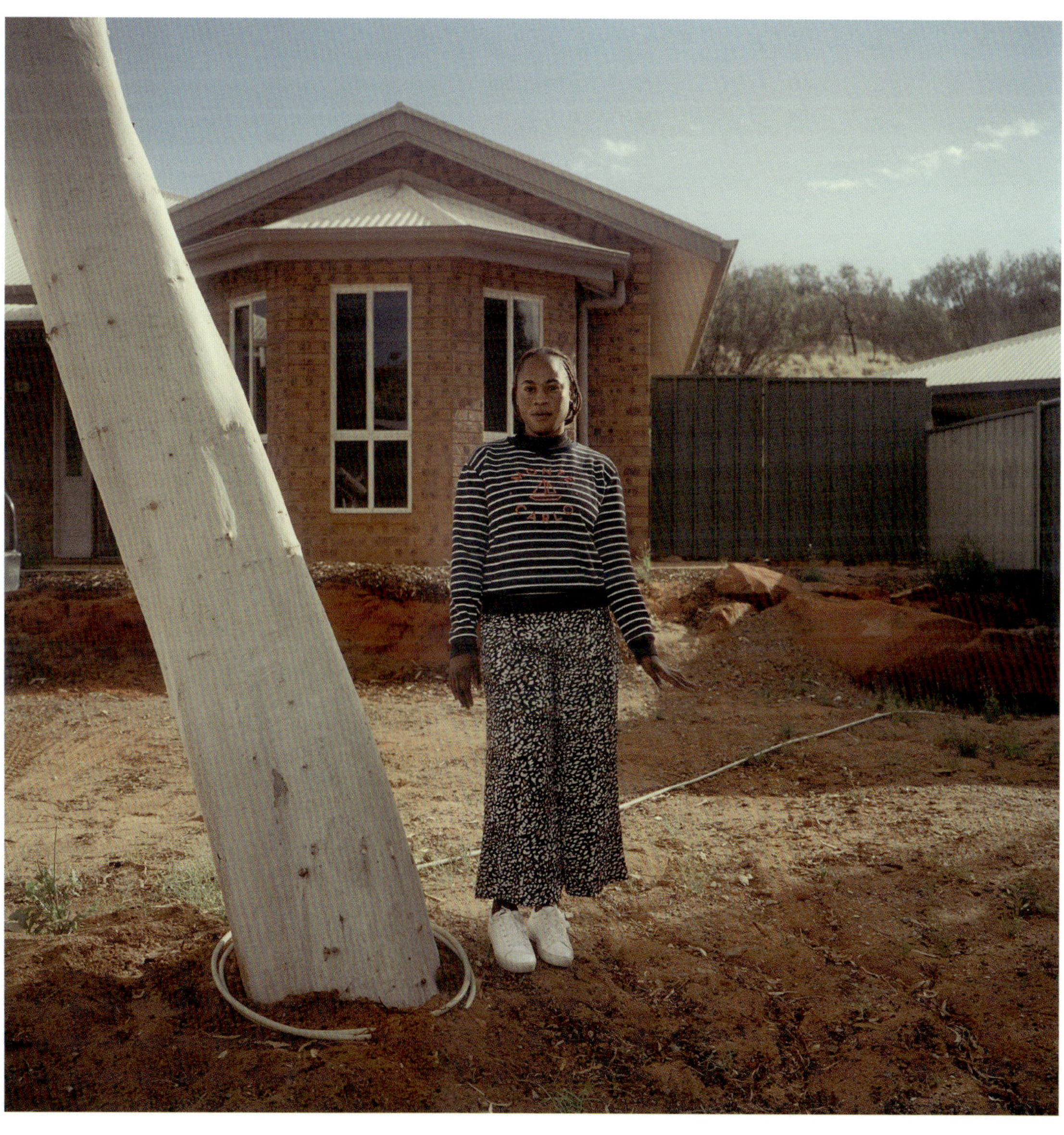

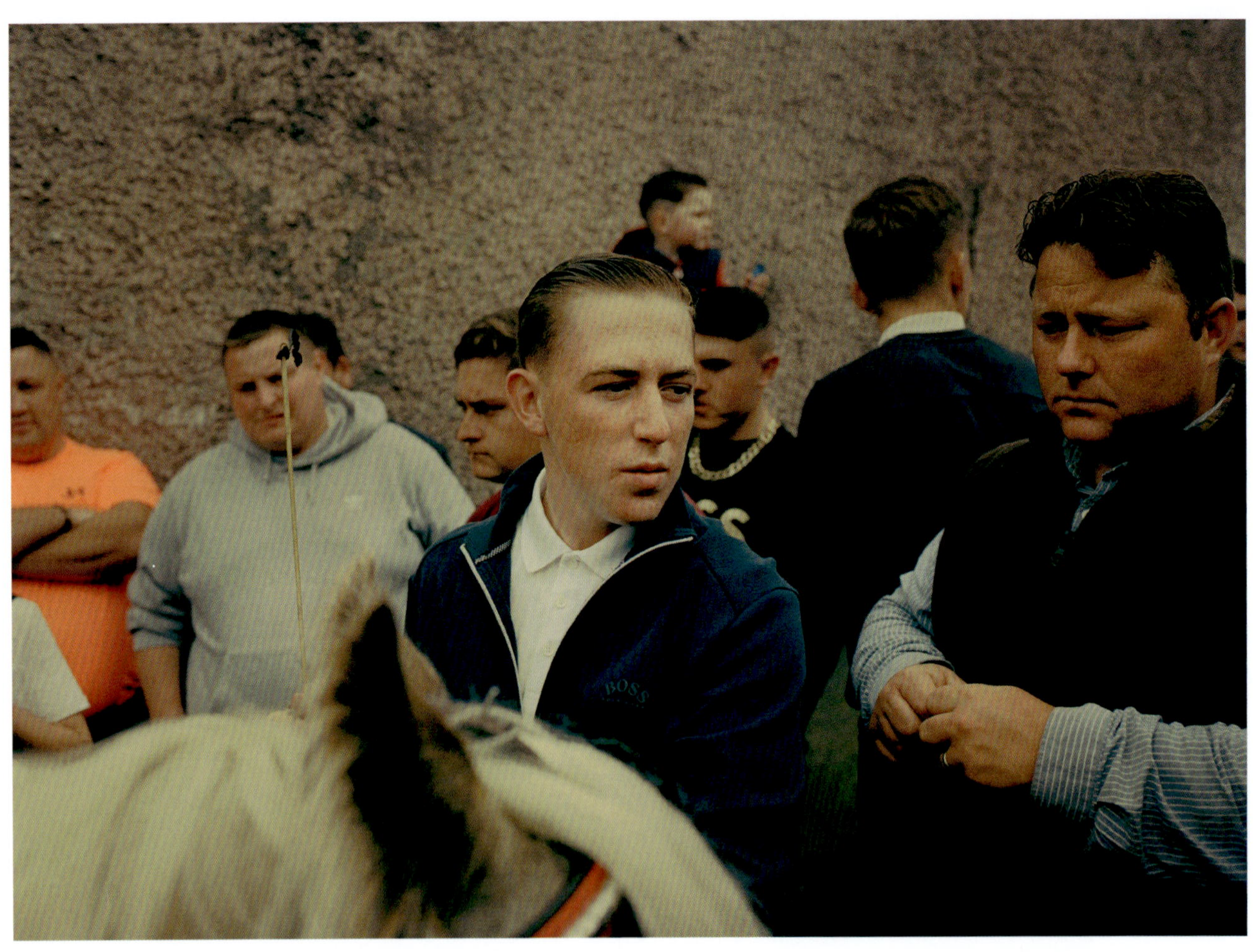

Sam Wright

Haggling at the horse fair, 2023
From the series *Pillar to Post*
Chromogenic print

Over two years, Sam Wright has immersed himself in traveller and gypsy communities from across the United Kingdom and Ireland; conducting interviews, meeting inspiring people and documenting through photography and film. Revisiting a family he had come to know, Wright positions himself with his camera amid the barter, capturing Jerry and Larry in this moment of traveller life – their composure seized within the hustle and bustle of the performative crowd-pulling horse fair at Buttevant, County Cork, Ireland. Horses are integral to the community, and the art of haggling is a tradition passed down through the generations.

Sarah Mei Herman

Ellen, 2023
Chromogenic print

This portrait occupies a space which can be considered both vibrant and tender. Sarah Mei Herman mentions her feelings of fascination with Ellen's appearance, alongside her positivity and strength. Ellen's attention to dress and detail makes for an eye catching portrait, making her life in her old age home all the more unexpected. The jewellery and lipstick stand in clear contrast to her backgrounds of delicate skin and soft fabric; the indirect gaze and shallow depth of field allow us to gaze at Ellen without distraction.

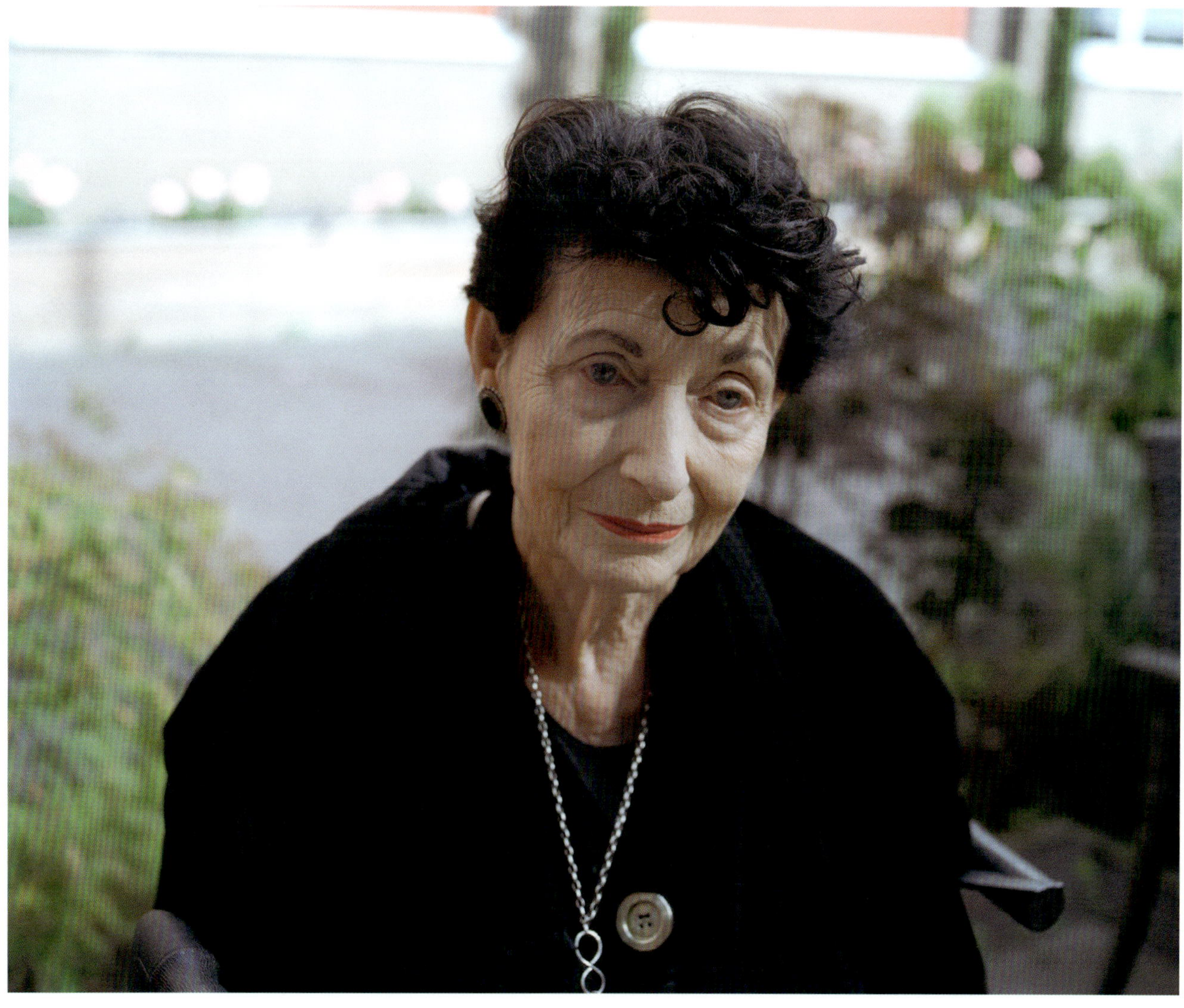

In Focus Photographer
Diana Markosian

Since 2015, the In Focus display has showcased new work by acclaimed photographers, including Hassan Hajjaj, Rinko Kawauchi and Pieter Hugo. Photographs by Diana Markosian, from her series and resulting published book *Father*, have been selected to be shown alongside the works in this years *Taylor Wessing Photo Portrait Prize*. This autobiographical project derives from a wider practice often driven by themes of family, community and belonging.

For most of my life, my father was nothing more than a silhouette in our family photo album.

Markosian did not set out to have a career with a camera; 'personal work is how I learnt to be a photographer' she says. Her wise images and poetic use of words belie her youthful 35 years. She was born in Moscow in 1989, to Armenian parents – a heritage which she explored through her 2015 series entitled *1915*. Through poignant portraits, landscapes and archival images, Markosian retraced the steps of survivors of the Armenian genocide 'to retrieve a piece of their lost homeland'. As a result, she found that stories concerning her own grandparents' escape from the massacres had context and connection. Markosian became an active participant in the survivors' stories, creating photographic billboards of their escape routes, offering a resolution that had been absent until then.

Markosian visualised and narrated her own childhood through the award-winning project *Santa Barbara*, which was exhibited and published as her first monograph in 2020. She 'excavated' and re-told her mother's biographical story that had been inspired by America, as depicted in the referenced soap opera. In 1996, when Markosian was seven, her mother Svetlana took her and her older brother to live in California, while her

father remained in Russia. It happened overnight. Markosian and her brother had no idea that they would be leaving their Russian childhood behind. Svetlana had advertised to meet someone who would become her husband, and Eli – Markosian's new 'dad' – like life in California, was at odds with the televisual portrayal.

Markosian described the project as a 'conversation with my mum' and a way to understand 'her decision to leave our culture, my father, and uncover the mystery around it all'. For this emotive revisiting, collaboration was necessary. Markosian worked with the original writer of the soap opera *Santa Barbara* and cast actors to re-enact her family's final days in post-Soviet Russia and their arrival in America. While deeply personal, universal themes are central to the story: desperation and bravery in the face of poverty, the idealised vision of life in California and the reality of the immigrant experience.

For Markosian, commissioned and personal work co-exist, informing one another. She discovered photography while studying for a master's degree at Columbia University's School of Journalism, New York; 'my desire was to see the world, and through photography I have been able to do that but in a more authentic way than I had anticipated.' Strengthening her love of photography, Markosian's mother helped her to buy her first camera. 'There is something very visceral about finding passion. And when you do it is almost like falling in love.'

Pursuing this as a career, Markosian moved to Moscow, aged 20. Her photographs from *Chernobyl* (2011), Ukraine, published in the *New York Times*, tell a moving story of endurance and love in the almost deserted villages of the 'zone of alienation'. On assignment for Bloomberg, Markosian was deported from Azerbaijan because of her Armenian heritage – at the time, the countries were at war

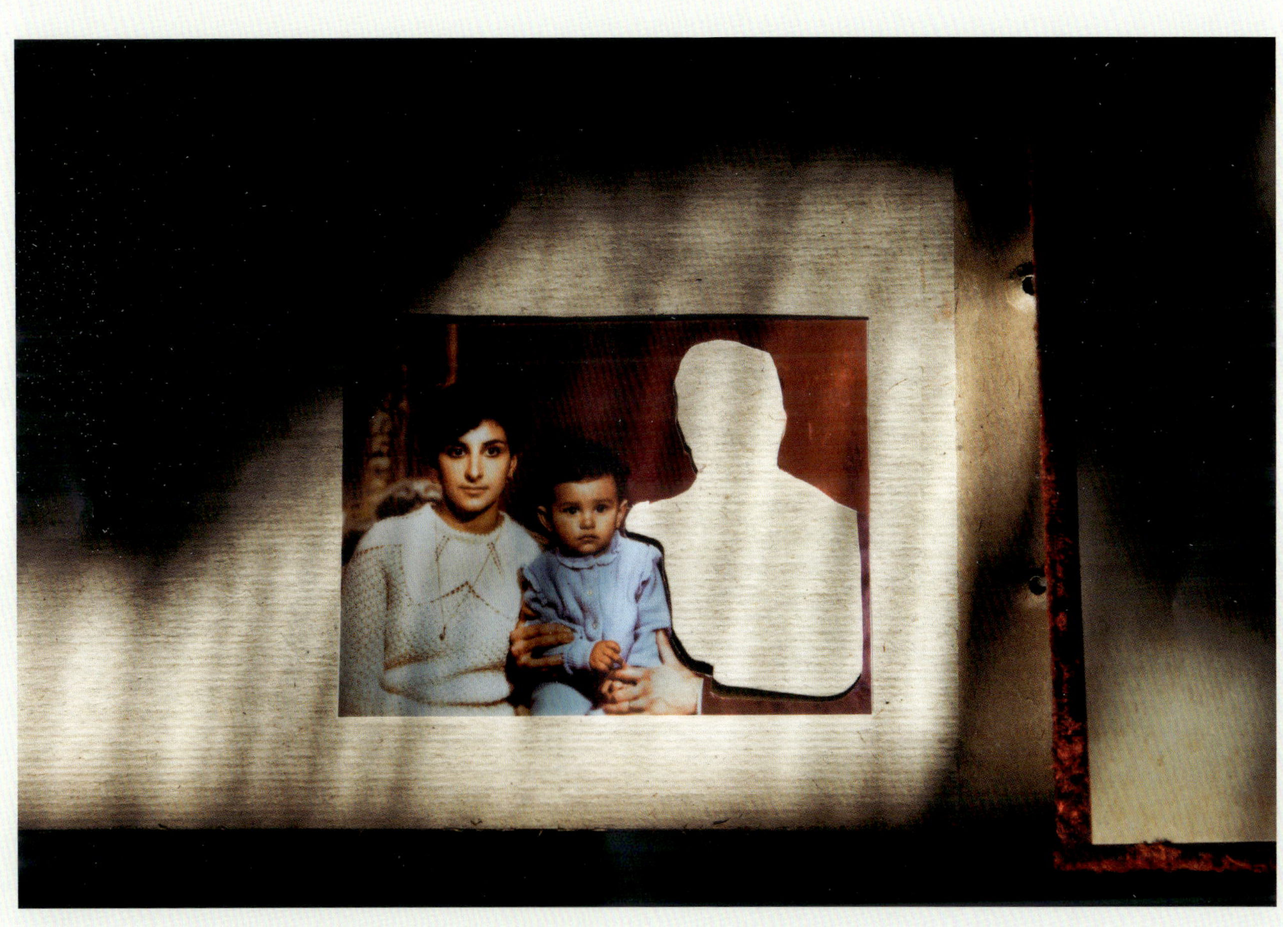

Diana Markosian

*My mother's photo album. The closest image I
had to my father. A cut out.*, 2015
Inkjet print

within the Nagorno-Karabakh conflict. She recalls, it was 'fascinating discovering who I am, through these consequences'. Work invited further travel for Markosian; on an assignment for *Time* magazine, she travelled to Chechnya, Russia. Over the course of two years, between 2011 and 2012, she depicted 'the lives of Chechen girls coming of age in a republic that is rapidly re-defining itself as a Muslim state in Russia'.

Aged just 23, Markosian gained her first assignment from *National Geographic* magazine. For this series, *Virgin Mary* (2015), she travelled to eight countries where she photographed 'Mary as a woman, a mother and as a global symbol who has influenced millions.' In each location, Markosian advertised for people, who claimed to have had visions of the Virgin Mary, to contact her. She photographed them and asked an artist to interpret their accounts. Markosian reflects how 'each one of these projects has changed me so significantly.'

In 2016 she became a Magnum nominee. Under the umbrella of this prestigious photography co-operative, through her photo essay *School No. 1* (2014), Markosian revisited the site of the Beslan school siege in Russia with former hostages. Her sensitive and powerful tribute, a decade on from the Islamic terrorist siege, was made through a combination of portraits, still life and archival imagery – only possible through Markosian's palpable empathy and great skill as a storyteller.

Four years following, Markosian immersed herself in a study of young migrants to Germany who were overcoming their fears through swimming lessons for her series *The Big Sea* (2018). Markosian worked with an art therapist to engage the children in visualising their journeys. 'I think you have to do more than just take an image. You need the drawings and interviews to bring in the views and feelings of the subjects'. The story that is told is a collaboration.

That same year, Markosian created the series *Quince* (2018), which was enabled by an Elliott Erwitt Fellowship Grant. For this project, in Cuba, she explored the coming of age through the quinceañera, the 15th birthday rite of passage into womanhood. 'A lot of my work is about the past and memory. It is less about going somewhere and more about finding my way into that country and my understanding of what that country represents for me'. Markosian found a parallel between her childhood backdrop of the collapse of the Soviet Union and the resulting economic hardship of 2010s communist Cuba. The quinceañera keepsake photobook, and the lavish celebration, is a constructed fantasy that Markosian explored by partnering with a local photo studio. She began to see the transition that girls were making to become women within Cuban society – the quinceañera was a marker of womanhood.

Most recently, Markosian has applied her powerful empathetic visual narration in a campaign with M&C Saatchi and the Archewell Foundation. It illuminates parents' experiences of the negative and often tragic impacts of social media on their children. For Markosian, photography is a collaboration wherever the project has taken place.

Exhibited in this year's In Focus display is Markosian's first iteration of her autobiographical project *Father*, which began in 2012 when she found her father, 15 years after her mother took the family to California. Markosian travelled with her brother to search for him. The resulting photographs culminated in a publication, where the images are accompanied with intimate yet concise poetic prose.

For most of my life, my father was nothing more than a silhouette in my family album.

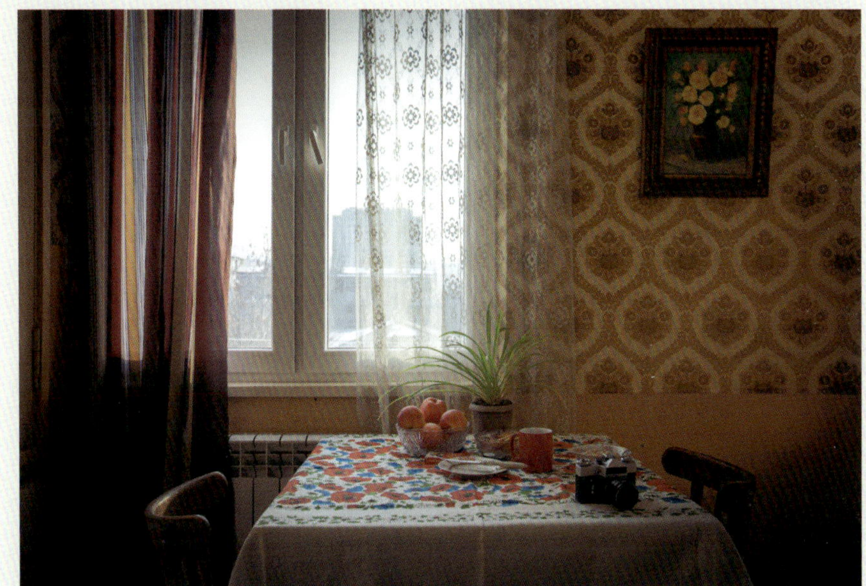

Diana Markosian
Monday, 2018
From the series *Father*
Inkjet print

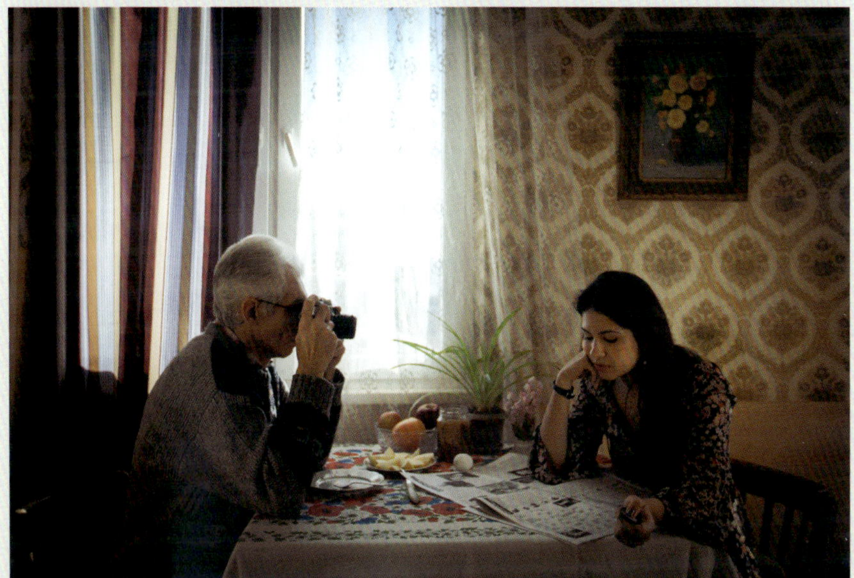

Diana Markosian
Friday, 2018
From the series *Father*
Inkjet print

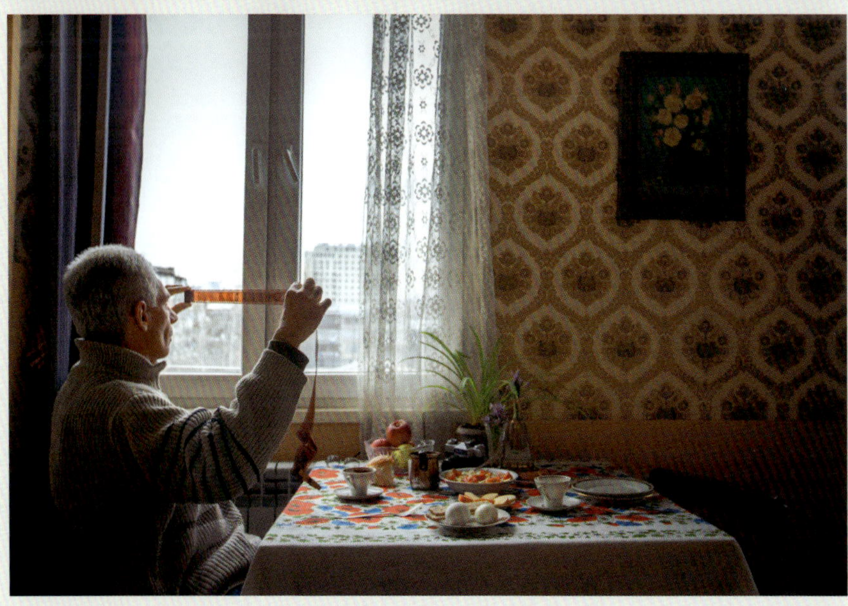

Diana Markosian
Sunday, 2018
From the series *Father*
Inkjet print

Diana Markosian
Father's photograph #1, 2018
From the series *Father*
Inkjet print

Diana Markosian
Father's photograph #2, 2018
From the series *Father*
Inkjet print

When I was 7,
My mother woke me in our apartment in Moscow
And told me to pack my belongings.
We didn't say goodbye to my father.

At first he didn't recognize me.
I didn't recognize him either.

Markosian and her father worked on building a relationship. She began to take photographs over time whilst staying with him. They tried to connect; through running together, the rare outing, breakfast. However, his frequent absences, due to a newborn daughter and therefore a new family, led Markosian to understand that she would have to reframe the reconciliation. Such a personal project has been both challenging and therapeutic – she has reached acceptance rather than a perfect outcome.

I often wondered what it would have been like to have a father.
I still do.

Father is the culmination of work compiled over a ten-year period. It is a journey of discovery whereby Markosian's father's search for his disappeared children is also revealed. Letters in Armenian and Russian written to 'embassies, police stations, toy stores, and random American addresses found in newspapers' are photographed in a suitcase:

Inside, a shirt for my brother's future wedding
and a collection of books for me.
Beneath them, hundreds of letters he had
written in search of us.
A newspaper clipping with my photo,
the words "missing child" printed over it.

The letters did not reach Markosian. Monochrome and colour photographs interspersed with family snapshots and Markosian's pinpoint prose convey underlying emotions. Exhibited here for the first time, Markosian 'did not see it as a project that I was going to finish. I just needed to understand my dad.'

The exhibit includes three photographs of the kitchen table, which Markosian framed through her camera when she would sit across from her father at breakfast. It was where the conversations took place, inviting viewers to be a witness of the evolving relationship. The decor is unchanged from decades past: 'His home was a museum of my childhood' Markosian writes.

Friday 10.17am – I ask you to take a picture of me.
Something you haven't done since I was 7.

In the last of the trilogy of table images, her father is looking at a strip of film – his own photographs. Two of them are included in this year's display. In one, Markosian is seen from behind looking at a cloudy sky. The enigmatic image is inscribed by her father to describe his own inner dialogue: 'A chasm of time has formed between us … I am trying to bring together the image of my little girl and my adult daughter today.' The other is cropped closely. Markosian's hand is wrapped in her father's and brought close to his mouth – the cold winter air just perceptible – as if he is holding on to her.

Quietly paced and narrated, the sequence of images in Markosian's publication of *Father* includes photographs featuring her grandfather, an artist, who dedicated much of his latter years to his failed pursuit of his missing grandchildren. Three monumental monochrome photographs anchor space in the exhibit, as if holding time still. In the first, ripples emerge from Markosian's hand

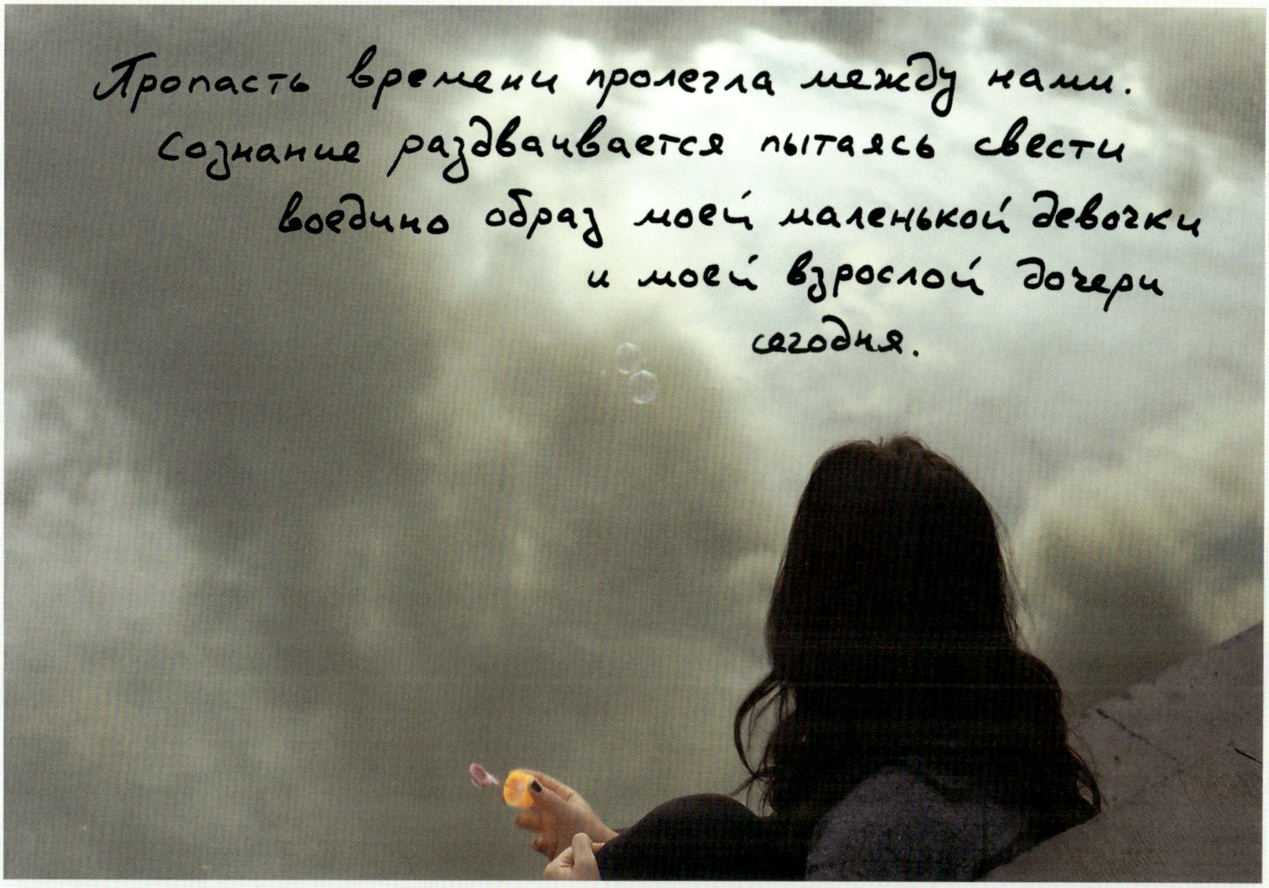

Пропасть времени пролегла между нами.
Сознание раздваивается пытаясь свести
воедино образ моей маленькой девочки
и моей взрослой дочери
сегодня.

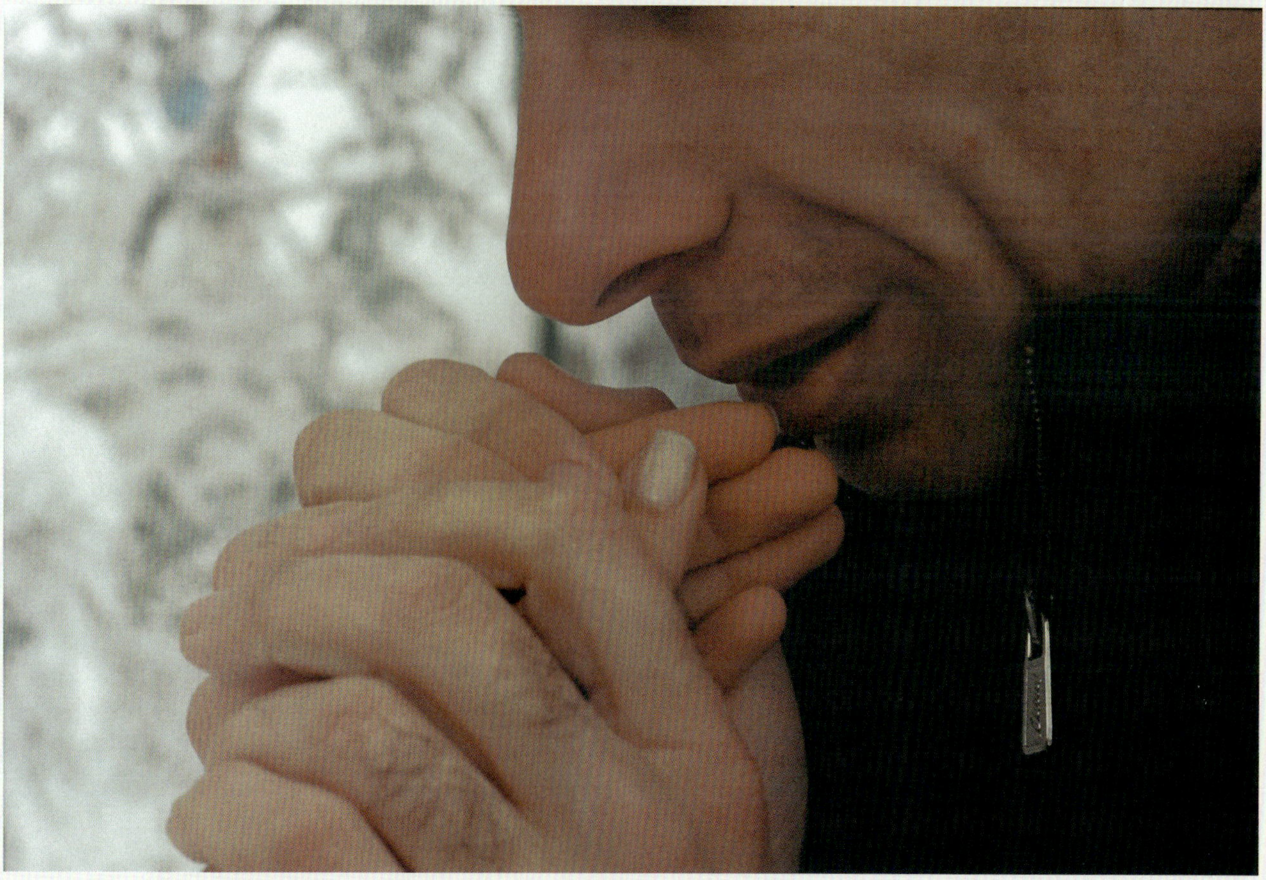

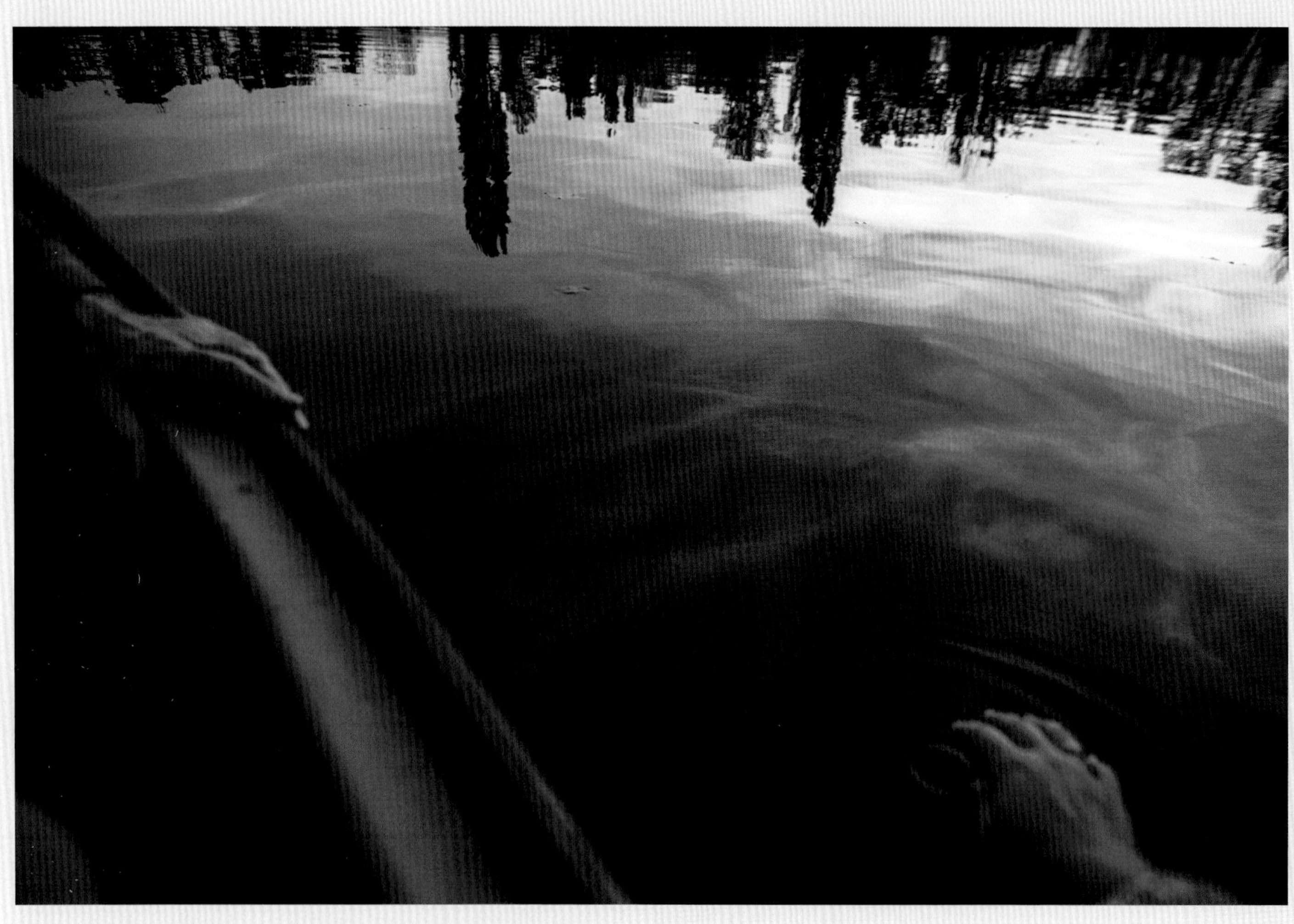

Diana Markosian
Together, Apart, 2015
From the series Father
Inkjet print

Diana Markosian
The Stranger, 2015
From the series Father
Inkjet print

Diana Markosian
My Father's Reflection, 2015
From the series Father
Inkjet print

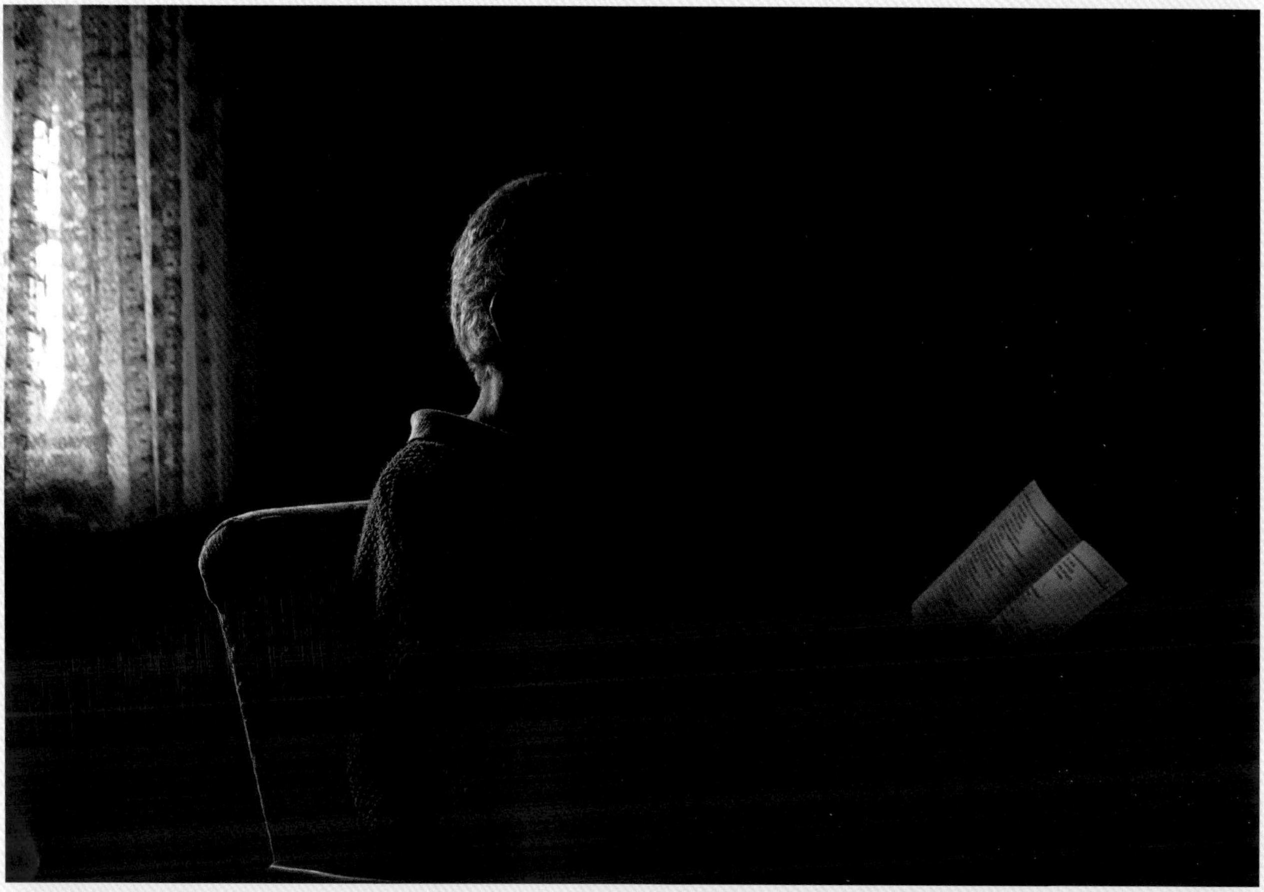

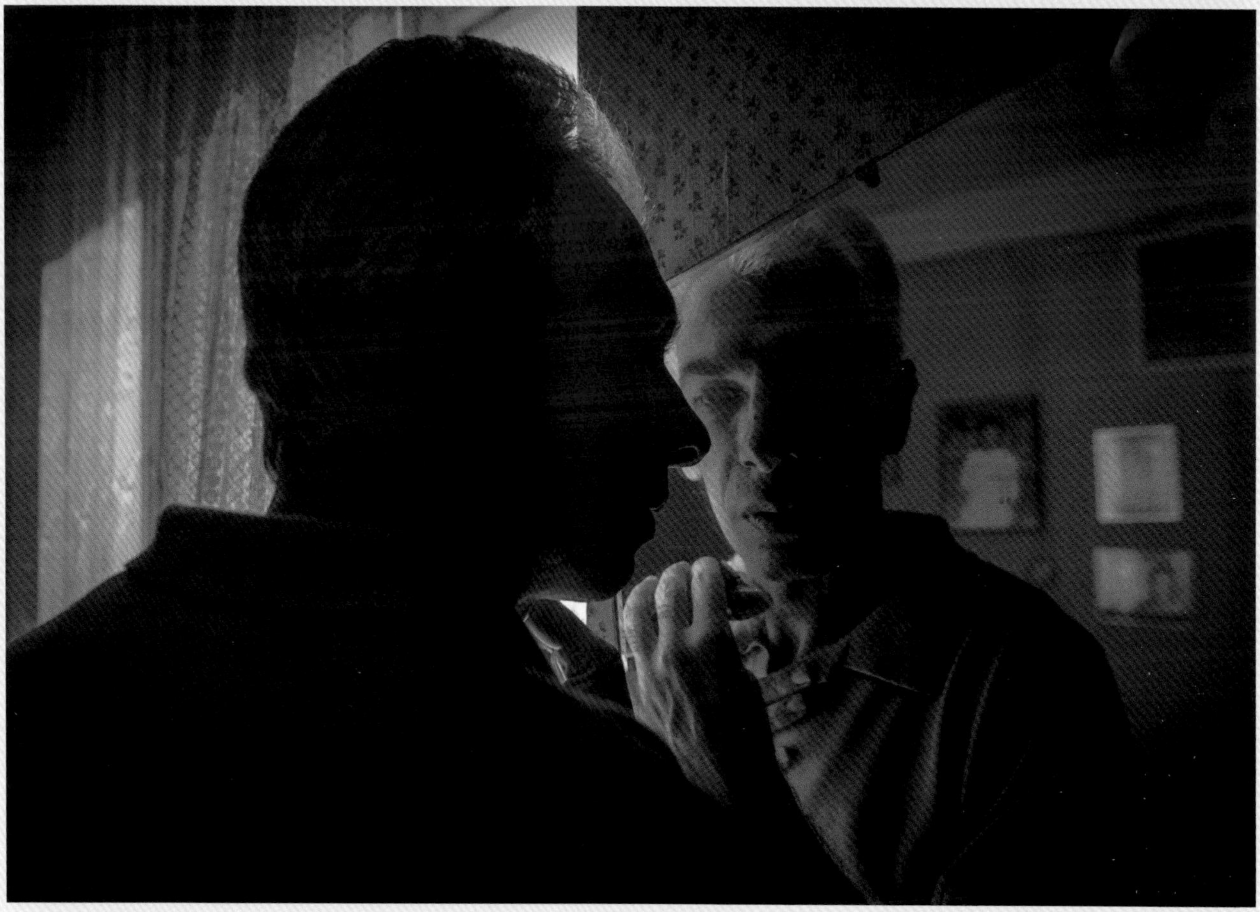

– a metaphor for how their reunion will be felt over time. In another, light from a window caresses her father who is reading, seemingly disappearing again into another world. In the final image, his face is revealed as he is shaving in a mirror, photographs of children pepper the wall behind, but his eyes are averted as if he is not fully present.

Markosian uses moving image as an extension of the book's narrative. She works with the cinematographer David Feeney-Mosier, drawing on archival film and recent footage of her father. As the thoughtful narrative of *Father* concludes, Markosian and her father's mutual airport farewell photographs succeed Markosian's resounding words: 'I keep searching for him; I think I always will.'

Markosian's ability to photograph things that are no longer there runs throughout her practice; whether deeply personal or in dialogue with an unfamiliar country or culture. Markosian acknowledges that finding a way to sustain life as a photographer is 'both a challenge and an excitement'. There has been a need for continual reinvention as expectations and budgets for commissioned work have shifted; and she has seemingly adapted. Markosian's powerful and unique way of storytelling has been published globally by *Vogue*, *Vanity Fair*, *The New Yorker*, and other aforementioned prestigious publications.

As an artist, she is represented by Galerie Les Filles du Calvaire in Paris, France, and Rose Gallery in Los Angeles, California. Through still photography, moving image, and collaborative authorship, Markosian's work can be defined as both conceptual and documentary. Her awards are numerous and feature at least one per year since 2012. Likewise, exhibitions have spanned cities including Istanbul, New York and Cardiff, and in institutions including the International Center of Photography, New York and the San Francisco Museum of Modern Art, where *Santa Barbara* travelled from its premiere at Les recontres d'Arles, France, in 2020.

The third and forthcoming chapter to the story, to follow *Santa Barbara* and *Father*, is in development as a feature length film with the plan to reunite her parents. It has been 30 years since they have seen each other, and they are willing participants – collaboration, once again, will be a critical and informative aspect of Markosian's meaningful and pervasive practice.

Interview by Clare Freestone